PREDYNASTIC EGYPTIAN POTTERY

in the Collection of the
Robert V. Fullerton Art Museum
California State University, San Bernardino

Julius D. Kaplan

Foreword by Eva Kirsch

Robert V. Fullerton Art Museum
California State University, San Bernardino
September 22, 2005 – February 18, 2006

2000 copies printed on the occasion of the exhibition
"Predynastic Egyptian Pottery
in the Collection of the Robert V. Fullerton Art Museum Collection,
California State University, San Bernardino"
at the Robert V. Fullerton Art Museum
California State University, San Bernardino
September 22, 2005–February 18, 2006

The exhibition and catalog have been funded by
California State University, San Bernardino
The Robert V. Fullerton Art Museum, Instructionally Related
Programs, Board of Associated Students, Inc., and private donors

Robert V. Fullerton Art Museum
California State University, San Bernardino
5500 University Parkway
San Bernardino, California 92407-2397

Exhibition Curator
Dr. Julius D. Kaplan

Exhibition Consultant
Dr. Diana Craig Patch

Museum Director and Exhibition Coordinator
Eva Kirsch

Museum Technician and Exhibition Designer
John Fleeman

Museum Staff
Sharidy Cunningham, Megan DeWitt, Catherine Aurora

Catalog Design: Thomas Ruvolo

Photography: Gene Ogami

Catalog printed by Faust Printing, Rancho Cucamonga

Library of Congress Cataloging-in-Publication Data

Robert V. Fullerton Art Museum.
Predynastic Egyptian pottery in the collection of the Robert V. Fullerton Art Museum, California State University, San Bernardino / by Julius D. Kaplan ; foreword by Eva Kirsch.
p. cm.
"Robert V. Fullerton Art Museum, California State University, San Bernardino, September 22, 2005-February 18, 2006."
Includes bibliographical references and index.
ISBN 0-945486-29-4 (pbk. : alk. paper)
1. Pottery, Egyptian--Exhibitions. 2. Pottery, Ancient--Egypt--Exhibitions. 3. Egypt--Antiquities--Exhibitions. 4. Pottery--California--San Bernardino--Exhibitions. 5. Robert V. Fullerton Art Museum--Exhibitions. I. Kaplan, Julius. II. Title.

NK3810.R63 2005
738.3'82'093207479495--dc22

2005024953

CONTENTS

Director's Foreword 4
Map of Predynastic Egypt 5
Introduction 6
Notes on The Catalog 11
B (Black-Topped Ware) 12
  Bowls 14
    Shallow Black-Topped Bowls 14
    Deep Black-Topped Bowls 20
  Beakers 26
    Black-Topped Beakers 26
  Jars 38
    Black-Topped Jars 38
    Black-Topped Jars with Small or Pointed Bases 50
P (Polished Red Ware) 62
    Polished Red Open Bowls 64
D (Decorated Ware) 86
    Squat Jars 102
Late Ware Jars 112
Stone Vases 118
Flint 122
Bibliography 126

DIRECTOR'S FOREWORD

Ancient Egyptian civilization has been fascinating people for more than two millennia. Long lasting and powerful, it left an astounding amount of material and written evidence. Today, we know a lot about ancient Egypt, but new discoveries reveal fresh material that allows exciting and stimulating interpretations – among them those tracking many of the elements of Dynastic Period of Egyptian civilization from the still much less known Predynastic Period – the period our museum's newest exhibition explores.

This small, well researched and splendidly displayed scholarly presentation of about 50 Predynastic objects, mostly pottery, from the museum's collection has been curated by Dr. Julius Kaplan, professor emeritus of art history at California State University, San Bernardino's department of art. The exhibition, on display at the museum from September 2005 until mid-February 2006, is the first in the three-part series of presentations and accompanying catalogs for the museum's permanent collection, dedicated to the entire history of ancient Egypt and planned for 2005-2012.

Ancient Egyptian art is the most remarkable part of the Robert V. Fullerton Art Museum's permanent collection. Close to 300 objects that encompass more than 4,000 years of ancient Egyptian history, represent all its main periods from Predynastic to Greco-Roman. Showing a variety of different themes, mediums and techniques used by the Egyptian craftsmen and artisans, the collection consists of various outstanding objects, including a life-size, anthropoid mummy coffin lid of Neter Heneb (650-300 BCE). About a quarter of the collection is now owned by the museum, with the balance on extended loan from the Harer Family Trust and Dr. Geoffrey A. Smith.

Most of the Predynastic collection objects presented in the exhibition have been donated to the museum by two passionate collectors, Dr. W. Benson Harer and Mr. Alan Lowy, whom I thank for their generosity and continuous support. Only a few objects included in the catalog are still on extended loan from the Harer Family Trust.

This exhibition - the result of thorough, scholarly research of the first portion of the museum's permanent holdings - is an important milestone in the life of our small museum. Its curator and my good colleague, Dr. Kaplan, deserves my most sincere appreciation for his dedicated, patient, and extremely valuable work on the exhibition's catalog and the willingness to continue his research for the planned future exhibitions of Egyptian art. Dr. Kaplan's long-time commitment, loyalty and continuous support for the museum have proven truly invaluable. His participation in many projects, including multiple exhibitions, educational programs and fund-raising campaigns has helped the museum to develop and grow stronger every year. I am extremely grateful for all Dr. Kaplan's contributions and I thank him for all his hard work.

Dr. Kaplan and I recognize that many others have contributed to the success of this project. We greatly value their involvement and thank them for their dedication and excellent work. In particular, we thank Dr. Diana Craig Patch, an expert on Predynastic pottery and assistant curator in the Egyptian Department of the Metropolitan Museum in New York. Her insights, information and advice have been truly invaluable during the process of writing the catalog, but any mistakes or misinterpretations are the sole responsibility of the author.

Students in the art department, Mieke Bahmer, Jeanne Ericson, Brooke Hess, Judy Solis, Mona Trippel and Amy Younger participated in the research for the entries where they are recognized. The work on this catalog could not have taken place without the constant assistance of Lee Bayer, head of Interlibrary Loan in the CSUSB's Pfau Library and her capable staff. We also thank Gene Ogami for the photographs of all the objects in the catalog, Sam Romero and Alan Lavore of the CSUSB's Public Affairs Department for their editorial work, Thomas Ruvolo for the catalog design, and John Fleeman for the innovative and extremely professional installation of the exhibition. The museum staff members, Cathy Aurora, Sharidy Cunningham and Megan DeWitt, helped with many aspects of the exhibition's organizational process, installation and opening reception. Sharidy Cunningham deserves very special recognition for patiently assisting Dr. Kaplan with his research materials. Robin Kaplan's editorial expertise was instrumental during all the phases of the catalog writing, professors Alan Smith and Erik Melchiorre of the CSUSB Department of Geological Sciences willingly identified some of the minerals from which the exhibition objects were made, and professor Tom McGovern was very keen to lend a hand and his photographic talents in an emergency situation.

The exhibition and catalog have been funded by California State University, San Bernardino and the Robert V. Fullerton Art Museum with some support from individual donors. Friends of the Robert V. Fullerton Art Museum, Department of Art, CSUSB Alumni Association and the Offices of the Dean and the Provost sponsored the exhibition's opening reception.

Thank you all,

Eva Kirsch, Director

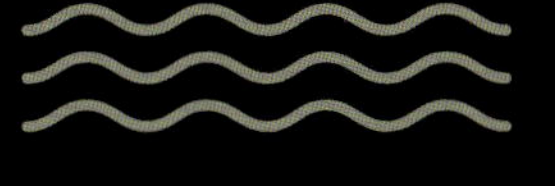

MAP OF PREDYNASTIC EGYPT

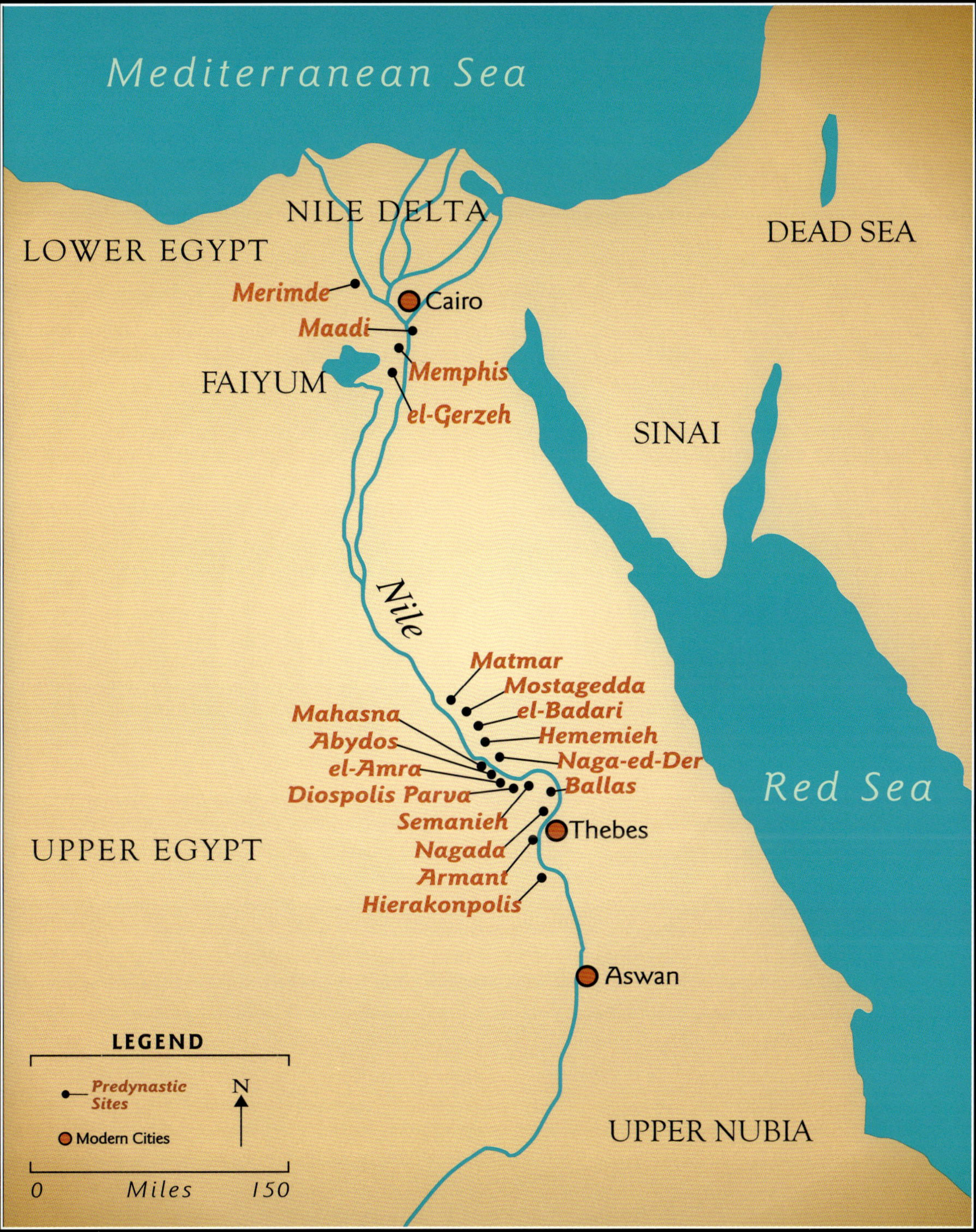

Mediterranean Sea
NILE DELTA
LOWER EGYPT
DEAD SEA
Merimde
Cairo
Maadi
Memphis
FAIYUM
el-Gerzeh
SINAI
Nile
Matmar
Mostagedda
el-Badari
Hememieh
Naga-ed-Der
Mahasna
Abydos
el-Amra
Ballas
Diospolis Parva
Red Sea
Semanieh
Thebes
Nagada
UPPER EGYPT
Armant
Hierakonpolis
Aswan

LEGEND
Predynastic Sites
Modern Cities
N
0 Miles 150

UPPER NUBIA

INTRODUCTION

The ancient Egyptians were hunters and gatherers for thousands of years before they began to practice agriculture and herding, collect into villages, and eventually form one of the most impressive cultures of human history. Their earliest surviving artifacts were practical tools made of flint and we assume that they also made woven objects of plant or animal fiber. As time passed these everyday items were buried with their owners for use in the afterlife, and eventually grew in refinement to become indicators of social status.

Fiber baskets, when not tightly woven, were coated with clay to improve their ability to carry tiny items, such as seeds. It is likely that one of these baskets fell into a cooking fire, or burned with a shelter, and then emerged as a hardened receptacle – pottery. Ceramics was a superior medium to basketry because of its impermeable and nearly indestructible nature. It can be broken when struck by or against a hard object, and may disintegrate over centuries of exposure to wind and water. But much of it remains intact or as small pieces. Pottery was used for storage, cooking, serving, eating and as containers to transport goods for trade. Whether found whole or broken in graves or as sherds in settlements, ceramic ware reveals much about the people who made it - how they lived, what they ate, what they believed and how they organized their world.

Ceramic and flint objects were made throughout the history of ancient Egypt but were at their finest in the Predynastic Period – the period before the development of writing and before the country was unified under a single political leader.

The clay used in most of these pots comes from the banks of the Nile River, where it was readily available. It is a dark silt that fires brownish-red. Initially each family or social group made objects for daily use. As the early Egyptians developed their skills at using fire, they must have noticed that the clay linings of their fire pits became hard and permanent after a number of uses. Once their cooking skills included baking, the firing of clay vessels could not be far behind.

Early Nile Valley pottery appears from at least 5000 BCE. In Lower Egypt, at Merimde, it was quite rough, while the Badarian pottery of Upper Egypt was so skillfully and beautifully made that we assume that those who made it were ceramic specialists. In addition to domestic use, ceramic vessels are found in the earliest graves and throughout Egyptian history to serve a need in the afterlife. At first these pieces were everyday ware, but eventually the best pieces – the pots that were perfectly symmetrical and balanced, with thin walls and elegantly simple surface treatment – became signs of status, probably made to be placed in graves. This practice lasted for more than a thousand years, until ceramic vessels were eventually replaced as luxury goods by those made of stone.

Around 3650 BCE towards the middle of the Predynastic period, a new kind of "marl" clay containing calcium carbonate appeared alongside Nile Silt. It fired to a buff color and required a high firing temperature that produced a hard fabric. The pots made from marl clay comprised fewer shapes than the previous Nile-silt ware, and were initially small, bulbous forms decorated with geometric designs, figures and other natural objects. Other depictions on larger vases, including incised pot marks added after firing, appear to be the earliest experiments with writing in ancient Egypt. These decorated pots, so similar to each other that they might have been produced in only a few workshops, were traded broadly along the Nile. (Trigger, 1983, p. 33) The fact that such similar vases are so widespread indicates that there was an audience with similar tastes and beliefs throughout the land. This speaks to an increasing unity of ideas, values and meaning – a social and political unity – as opposed to the earlier, disparate and more insular communities that existed along the river. (See Holmes, 1989, Friedman, 1994 and Kemp, 1989.) This pottery was made at the beginning of a political process that lasted about 300-500 years, which led to the unification of the country.

History of Predynastic Pottery

The discovery of Predynastic pottery and the scholarship surrounding it is full of surprises. While Egypt is the best preserved and most familiar ancient culture in the modern world (who has not heard of the pyramids or of the treasures of King Tut?), it is shocking to learn that until recently only a few Predynastic sites had their stratigraphy intact. That is, they had a clear set of layers of occupation from the earliest to the latest periods of the Predynastic. Undisturbed stratigraphy is essential for archaeologists and art historians in order to build a reliable chronology and picture of the culture, society and art of the people who occupied the area. A pot found in a specific archaeological layer relays a tremendous amount of information about the life of those who used it. But if that same pot is found in a disturbed site, or more likely in a dealer's showroom, it has lost its context and most of its ability to inform us about where and when it was made, and what it may have meant.

Another surprising aspect of Predynastic pottery is that it has been known for just over 100 years. In the 1890s Sir W. M. Flinders Petrie, an English archaeologist, excavated some 3,000 graves in and around the Upper Egyptian site of Nagada, which remains, along with Hierakonpolis, the largest and richest site of the Predynastic period. While isolated examples of similar material were known prior to his work, their vast number and variety recovered during his excavations made them appear to be something completely new. Petrie hypothesized that they were the products of a foreign people who invaded the Nile Valley after the Old Kingdom, but he soon changed his mind after reading the work of a contemporary archaeologist, Jacques de Morgan, who believed that this material was the product of a preliterate, indigenous culture that existed before the unification of Egypt.

Petrie was the first scholar to make sense of this rich and varied ceramic production. In a series of publications from the 1890s, culminating with a major study in 1921, he identified and organized this vast body of information and developed standards of identification that continue to be used in the scholarship of Egyptian ceramics. His Corpus identified nine types of pottery found in the graves: 1 – Black-Topped (B) ware, 2 – Polished Red (P) ware, 3 – Fancy (F) ware, 4 – White Cross-Lined (C) ware, 5 – Incised (N) ware, 6 – Wavy-Handled (W) ware, 7 – Decorated (D) ware, 8 – Rough (R) ware, and 9 – Late (L) ware. Petrie identified and organized the major shapes used for this pottery and its chronological development.

Much in his system is arbitrary. While the Corpus establishes standard types of pottery, Petrie admitted that no two handmade Predynastic pots were exactly alike. The Corpus drawings of pot types show perfectly flat bases and angular corners; however, the actual pots are much less precise. In organizing the Wavy-Handled pots, he developed a specific chronological order starting with an example he had purchased from a dealer, that is, a pot about which he knew nothing, which turned out to be from what is now Israel. For these and other reasons, many of his contemporary archaeologists refused to accept his system and scholars continue to take issue with his work. But over the past century, his Corpus has remained a basic tool for the study of Egyptian Predynastic ceramics. He has been proven correct in many of his basic assumptions about the sequential development of the pottery (Kaiser, 1957, Kemp, 1982), including his specific notions of how Wavy-handled ware developed. Scholars still refer to pots using his Corpus of shapes, and use some of his ceramic categories, especially Black-Topped, Polished Red, Cross-Lined, Decorated, Wavy-Handled and Rough ware. (Kaiser, 1957, Endesfelder, 1990, Patch, 1991, Crowfoot-Payne, 1992, Wilkinson, 1996 and Hendrickx, 2005 among others.)

Petrie also established the chronological development of the ceramics through seriation, or sequence dating, a system he invented and upon which his historical importance rests. In essence, he observed that certain pot types, such as Cross-Lined ware, were rarely if ever found with Wavy-Handled or Decorated ware. From this starting point, he developed an 18-step system in which he arranged different types of pottery chronologically. Obviously he could not give specific dates to this material, and he acknowledged that the development of pottery was irregular, probably slower at first and more rapid as time passed. He was able to use the ceramic evidence to establish a logically derived and reliable sequence. (But see Kaiser, 1957 and Hendrickx, 1996, pp. 36-38)

By the 1920s, Petrie was confident enough in his system to suggest three cultural and chronological phases, which he identified according to archaeological sites. The earliest was "Amratian" (from el Amra), the next "Gerzean" (from el Gerzeh) and the last "Semainian" (from Semanieh). One still finds this terminology in the literature, although most recent work follows Werner Kaiser's chronological divisions: Nagada I, II, III. Stan Hendrickx argued convincingly for this change, because Petrie's terminology implies three different cultures whereas Hendrickx believes that any phases are developmental stages of a single culture. (1996, p. 63) Even the major change in Nagada II to a uniform style and technique that Friedman (1994) noticed in the Rough ware pottery, Holmes (1989) in the lithics, and Patch (1991) in settlement patterns is seen as part of this developmental process. Some scholars, such as Williams (1987, 1988), go even further in seeing the seeds of every later development in ancient Egypt during this period, and argue that this is not Predynastic, but rather integrally related to the Dynastic. More recently Hendrickx, 2000, and Graff, 2003, have written iconographic studies supporting Williams' premise.

The idea of a common Predynastic culture first appeared in the 1950s in the work of Werner Kaiser, eventually the head of the German Archaeological Institute in Cairo. He also criticized Petrie, and made a name for himself by revising and clarifying Petrie's ideas about Predynastic pottery. (Kaiser 1955, 1957) He focused on the small, 170-grave cemetery at Armant, a carefully excavated and recorded site. He was the first to consider the location of the graves and their contents within the cemetery to establish a chronological development. He offered a more complex and nuanced development of this ceramic assemblage arranged in a series of 11 levels (stufen) and subdivisions that he named Nagada I, II and III. More recent studies developing notions of earlier and later parts of cemeteries have been made by Friedman, Payne and Hendrickx (Hendrickx, 2005, pp. 9-11), and Hendrickx' 1989 thesis (not seen) was the first to consider a full range of cemeteries in Upper Egypt to investigate the ceramics on a regional basis. Kaiser clearly states the notion of a single culture in the name (Nagada) he chose, and he was able to establish a subtle series of changing ceramic shapes that refined our knowledge of how the ceramics developed. Despite his critique of Petrie, his three categories match Petrie's earlier ones, so one finds references in the literature to Amratian/Nagada I, Gerzean/Nagada II and Semainian or Protodynastic/Nagada III. Thanks to radiocarbon and thermoluminescent dating, we now believe that Nagada I and early Nagada II lasted about 250 years (c. 3900-3650 BCE), Late Nagada II 350 years (c.3650-3300 BCE) and Nagada IIIa-b, that closest to and including the development of Dynastic culture, around 200 years (c. 3300 - 3100 BCE). (Hendrickx, 1996) While this chronological order is commonly used, Kaiser's conception of it has been questioned and refined by Hendrickx. (1996, p. 49 and note 21)

In the 1970s, there was an increasing interest in approaching Predynastic pottery from a "material" point of view. That is, establishing and classifying the different clays that were used, surface treatments, and all other "physical" aspects of the ceramics. This promised to be a more "objective" approach than the traditional one that focused on typology and decoration to establish chronology and function. (See Friedman 1994, pp. 82, 110, and 128-129 for the significance of tempering agents in creating this system.) The theory was that if one could discover and catalog this information, and then match it against mineralogical/petrological profiles of various geographical areas, then one could pinpoint the place where the pottery was made. Such identification would especially help in answering questions about trade, cultural contact and dating. To this end, scholars, including Dorothea Arnold and Janine Bourriau, following Nordstrom's study on Nubian ceramics (1972), began the work of establishing an updated and authoritative corpus of Egyptian pottery. To this end they created an organization (International Group for the Study of Egyptian Ceramics) and a journal. In 1982 a group of these specialists created the "Vienna System" that defined a number of types of silt and marl clays. (Nordstrom & Bourriau in Arnold, 1993, 168-186) Few examples they used were Predynastic and they recognized that their system was not an authoritative tool for studying the early pottery. Nonetheless this new approach created a standard for archaeologists, provided enough information to separate non-Egyptian from Egyptian ceramics, and prompted a number of chemical and geological studies. It has proved invaluable in studies of ceramic sherds from large geographic areas. (See below)

Since most studies of Predynastic ceramics involved objects taken from cemeteries, scholars were anxious to learn about the rich trove of ceramic fragments that characterized settlement sites. Remains from sites where people lived consisted almost exclusively of hundreds of thousands of sherds, and the cemeteries were full of them as well. Sherds, by their very nature, are much easier to analyze from a "physical" point of view. Since they are already broken and exist in such great number, studying the composition of their clay body, or even making fresh breaks for a clear view is not a problem. Following the model of the Vienna system, these scholars created their own corpus based on physical descriptions of the sherds. Hoffman and Berger at Hierakonpolis (1982, pp. 66-85) formed the first one (from 350,000 sherds they created 14 ware categories) and Friedman (1994) adapted their model in her study of Hememieh, Nagada and Hierakonpolis, Upper Egyptian sites that covered the entire Predynastic period. From 500,000 sherds she lists 16 types in her fabric/temper class, 12 of which are Nile Silt varieties, three are marl clay and one is unknown. Patch (1991), who conducted a surface survey rather than an excavation, chose another approach when she formed her corpus of Upper Egyptian Predynastic ceramics based on the shape and size of sherds first, then medium and decoration. She dated them based on a synthesis of the findings of Petrie, Kaiser and Kemp. Her results created an increased integration between the major chronological systems in use and allowed her to create specific and credible date ranges for most Predynastic pots.

In her 1994 Berkeley dissertation, Renée Friedman summarized the entire field of Predynastic ceramics, and for the first time offered a detailed analysis of settlement ceramics, as well as a thorough system of Predynastic clay types and pottery shapes. She was able to show, as Diane Holmes had in her 1989 thesis on stone tools, new information that offered a nuanced picture of the early Predynastic period. Dispelling the notion that from the beginning there was a unified culture leading to Pharaonic dynasties, Friedman found individual differences in some of the ceramics in the sites she studied. She discovered that in Upper Egypt, while there was similar Black-Topped and Polished Red ceramics at all sites in Nagada I, they each had different ways of making utilitarian pots that she called "kitchen-wares." Diane Holmes had presented evidence of a similar situation for flint tools. Friedman's settlement sherds revealed that in Upper Egypt from the time of the earliest settlements, a kind of rough silt functional ware was made that differed in its makeup from community to community. This material had been ignored because insignificant amounts of it appeared in graves and it was overlooked among the thousands of sherds at the settlement sites. She discovered that it was only around 3650 BCE, in the middle of the Nagada II period that this variety of "everyday" ceramics was replaced by a technically uniform chaff-tempered pottery throughout Upper Egypt, the kind that Petrie called Rough ware. (Friedman, 1994, 1-2) This is exactly the time (Nagada IIc-d) that Patch discovered evidence of the first clustering of settlements (1991, p. 334), which is the crucial beginning when a pre-state society undergoes changes that over a period of several hundred years lead to state formation. (Patch, 1991, p. 361) Wilkinson (1996) used a computer seriation study to explore regional differences between Predynastic settlements. The discoveries of Friedman, Holmes, Patch and Wilkinson have social, economic and political ramifications, such as suggesting a system of manufacturing and trade that was eventually controlled from the top, led by a single economic/political power. Wilkinson (1994-95, 1996, 2000) proposes a scenario for this development, that he calls "state formation". (See Hendrickx, 2005, pp. 4-11 for the most authoritative discussion of the history of research on Predynastic – Early Dynastic chronology.)

Function

The very early Predynastic coarse, utilitarian ceramic ware Friedman discovered in the settlements were probably food containers. That such ware predominates in the settlements is to be expected since people could make what they needed. In the Badarian and Nagada I periods, when the ancient Egyptians lived in the flimsiest of wattle-and-daub huts, cooking and eating outside, probably sitting on mats around the cooking pot, they made extremely thin-walled, beautifully crafted Black-Topped and Polished Red vessels. Evidently they found this ware beautiful and pleasing, and small amounts of it as well as slate palettes were found in most graves in Upper Egypt. Black-Topped pottery and perhaps some Polished Red ware has been found in the early Lower (northern) Egyptian site of Maadi (Rizkana and Seeher, 1987, pp. 29-30, 66), where what were relatively common objects in Upper Egypt proved to be attractive and were thus valued as trade goods.

The earliest shapes were simple open bowls and cups, larger ones for food and smaller ones for drink. Pots with curved bottoms conduct heat evenly as was appropriate for cooking; the shallower, open forms allow food to cool more quickly, higher walled vessels keep food hotter longer. Pots were made with large openings so that people could get things into and out of them, whether during the process of cooking, serving or eating. Many vessels had round or pointed bottoms to stabilize them as they rested in the sand, and they often show clear signs of such usage and wear. Most people used shells from the various Nile bivalves as eating utensils. (Friedman, 1994, pp. 240-262)

The simple, open utilitarian forms of early Nagada I Black-Topped and Polished Red ware were found in settlements (Patch, 1991) and in graves. (Friedman, 1994, p. 543) Petrie and most subsequent experts believe that over time the potters began to create shapes with curved sides and smaller openings at the top to form storage vessels. By the end of Nagada I, c.3800 BCE, defined lips were added to the openings of the vessels, which makes it easier to pour from them. Of course, there is an aesthetic dimension to such a development as well; it indicates a change from focus on the overall shape of the vessel to an interest in constituent parts and detail, such as the lip and spatial relationships.

When not in use, these ceramic objects were probably kept in pot stands, stacked out of the way or hung to avoid breakage. Living space was not rigidly controlled in the early settlements and undoubtedly pots were easily damaged. As is common practice in our time, cheaper ware was used everyday and the best pottery was reserved for special occasions, which in Predynastic times often meant for funerals, as grave goods. But as time passed, Black-Topped and Polished Red ware were fairly common even though for the first 250 years of Predynastic culture graves contained only one or two pots, and it was not until around 3650 BCE that there was an average of five pots per grave. (Kaiser, 1957, p. 72)

One needed to take appropriate vessels for cooking and eating into the grave, and we assume that this means they believed in an afterlife. In Dynastic times those who could afford to were focused on preparing for the afterlife. Since the Predynastic Egyptians buried their dead with objects, we can assume they had spiritual beliefs and religious rituals. While we have little information about the exact nature of their religious activities, we can assume that there were funerary repasts or special meals to celebrate events such as successful hunts, solstices, harvests, etc. It may have been appropriate to use the best ware for such occasions.

Context

An important issue in understanding Predynastic ceramics is the social and political context in which it was made. There are still many questions about the exact nature and development of Predynastic society, but scholars such as Hofmann, 1980 (revised 1991); Kemp, 1989; Kaiser, 1990; Patch, 1991; Wenke, 1991; Bard, 1994; Wilkinson, 1999 are beginning to clarify the steps by which primarily small hunting and gathering groups developed into ever larger and more complex communities, created trading relationships with each other and eventually formed alliances that resulted in independent political regions, one of whose leaders eventually founded a single state with a written language and a common religion. Some scholars, such as Bruce Williams, believe that important clues and evidence for this reside in the artifacts that remain, especially the ceramics. And an argument has been made that the pot marks and decorations on Predynastic pottery are the beginnings of the development of Egyptian hieroglyphics (Arnett, 1982). (See also the articles by Hendrickx, 2000 and Graff, 2003 mentioned above.)

NOTES ON THE CATALOG

In identifying the pots in our collection we have used the following definitions from Millett, 1979, p. 37:

Dish – a shallow vessel whose height is less than one-third its rim diameter

Bowl – a vessel whose height is more than one-third, but less than its rim diameter

Cup – a small version of a bowl (not defined in Millett)

Beaker – a vessel whose height is greater than its rim diameter; and which is of suitable size and shape for drinking from

Jar– a vessel with a neck, whose rim diameter is less than its height

Flask – a vessel with a neck very narrow in comparison with its height and girth

Storage jar – a jar so large that it seems unlikely to have been frequently moved when full.

We follow Petrie's typology of Predynastic pots that is B ware (Black-Topped), P (Polished Red), D (Decorated). In addition we will also refer to Federn's revisions to Petrie (see Needler, 1981) for what he calls B1 – bowls with polished black interiors and red outside, and P2 – half-polished bowls with red slip on wall on interior and just below the rim on exterior.

Dimensions are in inches and centimeters and include height, rim diameter (indicated by the word "rim," measured from the outer edges), the widest part of the vessel, and base diameter, indicated by the word "base." Normally the proportional relations recorded are width to height, rim to height and base to height.

The fabric identification follows that of Janine Bourriau in her 1981 Cambridge exhibition in which all Black-Topped and Polished Red ware is made of Nile Silt and all Decorated ware is made from marl clay.

Dates are approximate at best, and our system synthesizes that of the most recent scholars, which are based on a small number of generally accepted carbon 14 dates. [Hassan (1984), Patch (1991), Friedman (1994), Hendrickx (1999)]. We have chosen to follow the chronology published in Hendrickx 1996 (although he now dates the Nagada periods fifty years earlier – 2005, p. 26) as well as utilizing his Nagada I, II, III classification

Badarian	ca. 4400 – 3900 BCE SD (Sequence Dates) 21-29
Nagada I – IIa-IIb	ca. 3900 – 3650 BCE SD 30-44
Nagada IIc-IId (Late Nagada II)	ca. 3650 – 3300 BCE SD 45-64 (appearance of Wavy-Handled ware, and first time average number of vessels in graves reaches five)
Nagada IIIa-IIIb	ca. 3300 – 3100 BCE SD 65 - 75

Petrie's Corpus provides sequence dates for a large number of the pots he illustrates, and despite recent doubts about their accuracy (Hendrickx, 2005, p. 6) we use them as a starting point in our discussions to give historiographic perspective on the problem of dating. We will rely on the more recent specialized chronological studies: Kaiser (1957), Endesfelder (1990), Patch (1991), Payne (1992), Hendrickx (1996), Wilkinson (1996), and Hendrickx (2005). Diana Patch's personal communications about dating were based upon Stan Hendrickx's work for "The Relative Chronology of the Naqada Culture: Problems and Possibilities," in Spencer, 1996, pp. 36-69. When pots like those in our collection appear in these sources with sequence dates, we use them all, even when they reach the same conclusions, to build the evidence for a secure chronological placement.

Objects in the exhibition that are the property of the Harer Family Trust are indicated by an asterisk (*) before the title.

B (BLACK-TOPPED WARE)

Black-Topped ware is among the earliest and finest of Predynastic ceramics as well as the most prolific from c. 4400-3650 BCE (Nagada I-IIb), although it was occasionally found in the Early Dynastic period. It is completely hand-built, often with relatively thin walls. It appears in the earliest graves and settlements and the finer pieces seem to have been valued from the beginning. There are frequent examples of mended pots, suggesting that they were special enough to preserve. (Ayrton and Loat, 1911, pl. XXVI, no. 6) The ware is striking: the black is often luminescent and the red rich and shiny; the interior is often black as well. The forms of the best pieces are so perfect that one might mistakenly assume they were wheel-made, and against the clear and elegant profiles, the irregularity of the black at the top of the vessel makes an impressive contrast. Their elegant and spare shapes combined with the free composition of their decoration make most experts deem them second only to the even more exquisite Badarian rippled ware as the finest pottery made in the entire history of ancient Egypt.

All the various processes of hand-building were used to create these vessels: molding (often the base would be molded from another jar or a ceramic or wooden form), coiling (the coils would then be added to the base) and hand-turning (on some sort of mat or movable surface), usually for the rim. Other processes were hand-pinching (usually for smaller objects), slab construction (used in place of or in addition to coils) and paddling (beating the clay walls against some sort of surface to smooth and thin them). Most are burnished, in which case the marks indicate the physical process of making the pot. The vertical marks reveal the movement of the potter's hands as he drew upward on the clay coils, transforming them into walls. Likewise, the horizontal burnishing around the rim repeats the turning process by which the vessel was made. The earliest examples were baked in a bonfire, but the potters quickly learned to control the fire enough to make this fine and elegant ware, apparently by covering it with dung or mud. (Baba and Saito, 2002). This process tends to produce a gray surface on the interior of the pot. (Friedman, 1994, p. 181) By requiring further work after firing, these pots involve a more sophisticated control of the medium than solid color pots, and that may be why there are fewer of them than the Polished Red ware. Once the pot is made, it has to be taken out of the fire and turned upside down into material that shuts off oxygen to the part of the pot it covered, turning it black, sometimes on the surface and sometimes all the way through. These pots all look the same; that is, they have a reddish body and a black top so in that sense there is an accepted style, but the shape and position of the black along the top is random.

While one can explain this ware in technological terms, Arkell, 1960, used an anthropological explanation by suggesting that it imitates the gourd cups and bowls of African people to the south, especially Nubia. These gourds were singed around the edges, which evidently strengthened them to prevent chipping and breaking. When people accustomed to the look of such vessels moved to making them from clay, they brought this aesthetic along with them. And high-quality Black-Topped ware continued to be made in Nubia for a thousand years after it was no longer produced in Egypt.

Elizabeth Finkenstaedt (Cleveland, 1985; JARCE, 1985) speculates that environmental or cultural reasons explain such technological choices; that is, artisans and consumers enjoyed and favored red and black because these colors meant something to them. It must have been meant for use on important occasions both in life and in the afterlife. Later the Egyptians spoke of their environment in two basic terms. They referred to the rich, dark, cultivated land of the Nile valley and delta as the "black" land, and to the dry, surrounding desert as the "red" land. Even though our pots come from a preliterate period whose citizens left no evidence of their thoughts except as contained in the objects themselves, the strong resemblance of the basic color choices of these pots with the later conceptual division of the land of Egypt suggests a possible connection. The fact that the use of these two colors in pottery disappears after the Predynastic period may be because in Egyptian Dynastic art there were other, more effective means of expressing the dualities of the Egyptian environment.

(The starting point for this essay was Brooke Hess' seminar report, CSUSB, 2004.)

SHALLOW BLACK-TOPPED BOWLS

Nile Silt

Nagada I – II c. 3900 – 3300 BCE

Three similar bowls in the collection are equivalent in size to a modern, small dessert saucer that fits easily in one hand and is very functional. The bowls differ in that one has a round bottom and two have a flat base. All have black interiors that were originally shiny and red exteriors. Open form vessels always have finished interiors, since they are visible when used. We are calling bowls like this Black-Topped, but they have been seen as a distinct class of Predynastic pottery that falls between the B and P ware. Federn in Needler isolated this as a specific ware category when he revised Petrie's system, calling it B2. (1981, p. 70) There are examples where this color choice is reversed. There is also ware that is all black or all red. All these varieties are made from Nile Silt. Was there a reason for these color choices, did they mean anything? Were specific foods served in special bowls, did the color choices imply specific functions?

These bowls reveal clear vertical, horizontal, angular, hatched and cross-hatched burnishing patterns. Such rhythmic movement on these small, functional bowls may simply be a question of taste, keeping them interesting visually. Or, these patterns may have meant something, raising the same questions asked above about the color arrangements.

We are so accustomed to perfect potting that the irregularities in the dimensions of these bowls are worth mentioning. They may be due to heavy use, as suggested by the gouges and chips on the bottom. More likely they are the result of the high demand for such functional ware, which does not require careful potting.

Bibl:
Petrie, 1921
Kaiser, 1957
Needler, 1981
Patch, 1991
Payne, 1992

1. Black-Topped Shallow Bowl
Museum No. 03.019.2000

Height: (irregular) 1 5/8 to 1 3/4" (3.2 – 4.4 cm.)
Rim: (irregular) 4 5/8 to 4 3/4" (11.7 – 12 cm.)

With its completely rounded bottom and smooth rim, this is similar to P1a in Petrie's Corpus, with a sequence date of 32-54, 78, and could have been used as a scoop. It has horizontal burnishing at the rim. On the red exterior is a burnishing pattern made up of a design like a large parenthesis, with each side repeated several times, and over this pattern are a series of horizontal lines, producing a hatched effect.

A thick, opaque black resin or paint applied over the interior surface and rim is a modern addition. (Calinescu)

Date

While Petrie places the Corpus bowl in Nagada I and II and even one level of III, all subsequent experts have limited it to I and/or II. Kaiser (1957, p. 73) mentions that at Abydos a simple round bottomed small cup (P1a) appears in Ia (c.3900-3800). Patch (1991) dates this type of pot to IIb – IId1 (pp. 479, 491, pl. 15). Payne (1992, pp. 186, 188) places similar bowls in Ic, IIa and IId2, and in 1993 to Ic (p. 64, cat. 434). Hendrickx, 1996 places it in both Ia and Ib, and argues against making the distinction between these two levels since they are so similar; but in 2005, he dated it in Ib (p. 12). The conclusion is that this was a characteristic functional type of Predynastic vessel.

Coll. Lowy

Bibl:
Lowy catalog, pp. 19-20, No. 19
Payne 1993
Hendrickx, 1996
Hendrickx, 2005

2. Black-Topped Shallow Bowl
Museum No. 03.021.2000

Height: (irregular) 2 1/2 - 2 3/4" (6 – 6.5 cm.)
Rim: 5 15/16" (15.2 cm.)
Base: 1 1/2" (3.8 cm.)

This bowl has horizontal burnishing marks, and is irregularly blackened on the exterior over the simple rim. Some areas of black are outside the rim area. There are places on the interior and rim where one can see the reddish color of the clay where the black did not take during firing. The red exterior is quite worn, but some remnants of red burnishing and horizontal burnishing marks are visible. Its proportion of height to diameter is 1:4.

Date

In the Corpus, B11a is close, if a bit smaller, with a sequence date of 35 to 61, which covers Nagada I, II and early III. Also the Corpus example has a flat bottom, and despite appearances to the contrary, our bowl does too. This bowl can rest in a stable position, and the base surface is missing due to heavy use. Related bowls are in Kaiser (1957) in Nagada Ia,b,c and IIa. Patch (1991) dates B11a, described as having straight sides and a plain, everted rim, to I - IIab (pp. 453, 465, pl. 1, #14) and Payne, 1992, p.188 suggests a later date of IId2. Wilkinson, 1996, identified this type of bowl in tomb 1632 at Mostagedda in the second of his pottery sequences (p. 50), dating no later than IIb at this cemetery (p. 49).

Coll. Lowy

Bibl:
Lowy catalog, p. 20, No. 21
Wilkinson, 1996

3. Black-Topped Shallow Bowl
Museum No. 01.003.2003

Height: (irregular) 2 3/8 – 2 1/2" (c. 6 cm.)
Rim: 5 3/4" (14.5 cm.)
Rim thickness: 1/4" (.7 cm.)
Base: 2 1/16" (5.5 cm.)

This bowl's balanced shape is created by proportions of height to rim of 1:2.5 and base to height of 1:1. With its angular sides, it fits nicely in one hand or two, so its shape makes it a perfect vessel for eating.

Trippel suggests that it may have been used for food preparation since it is so worn on both interior and exterior. Cooking outside on a sandy surface where using the bowl would press it against the earth could explain the abraded exterior surface and uneven base. Black drops appear around the rim and may be some sort of resin, which also covers the interior and is a modern addition. (Calinescu)

A unique feature of this pot is a precise round black circle in the middle of the base. It appears to be below the surrounding red surface, so it may have been made by something covering the pot during firing. Pot marks appear on the base of Predynastic pots and this circle may be intended to identify the potter.

B11 is the closest parallel in the Corpus. (See entry above.)

Coll: Harer

Bibl:
Scott, 1992, cat. No. 2C, p. 14
Mona Trippel, Seminar Report, CSUSB, 2004

DEEP BLACK-TOPPED BOWLS

The collection contains three similar deep bowls and a cup that is simply a smaller version of them. All are of the same material, manufacture and use, and share a proportion of base to rim of 1:2. The bowls are evenly proportioned, have a tapering shape, simple rims, fairly thick walls, and sit on wide, flat bases. They fit nicely in two hands, and appear to be functional eating vessels. Their bases provide solid support, and all have wear on the lower third and bottom and chipped rims that indicate heavy use.

They have iridescent black over the top part of the exterior that sometimes carries over the top of the interior. The rest of the exteriors were originally shiny red. Most of the interiors are rough at the bottom but smoother on the walls.

As one would expect for such a functional shape, they seem rapidly made, roughly smoothed on the bottom as if mold-made with a pressed or paddled upper wall. Often horizontal smoothing and tool marks appear on the walls on the interior, whose color is brown Nile Silt, covered with gray, black or a combination of both – typical for vessels whose interiors are visible.

Date

They all date I-IIb c. 3900-3650 BCE. This type of open vessel was among the earliest of the B ware. Wilkinson calls this type a medium-sized deep beaker bowl. (1996, p. 105) Petrie placed these vessels in Nagada I and II, and Kaiser charts a B18 k vessel to Ib (1957, pl. 21) and Patch, 1991 places it in I-IIb. (pp. 454, 466, pl. 2) Since Patch's date is based on sherds, it can be narrowed when dealing with whole pots. (Patch, personal communication). Payne dates this type to IIa, (1992, p. 186) and in 1993 to Ic. (p. 36, cat. 132)

Nile Silt

Coll: Lowy

Bibl:
Petrie, 1921
Kaiser, 1957
Patch, 1991
Payne, 1992
Payne, 1993
Wilkinson, 1996

4. Black-Topped Deep Bowl
Museum No. 03.006.2000

Height: Irregular 4 3/8 to 5 1/8" (5" = 12.6 cm.)
Rim: 6 3/16" (15.4 cm.)
Base: 3" (7.6 cm.) not completely flat

With proportions of base to height of 1:1.6 and base to rim of 1:2, it is most like B18c in the Corpus, which Hendrickx, 2005, dates to Ib (p 12). It must have been very attractive when it was new, with nearly perfect symmetry.

Iridescent black is applied to the top inch of the interior so regularly that a brush was probably used. The exterior is diagonally burnished and reveals a diagonal tool or finger mark near the rim and ridges from the forming and smoothing process are visible on the interior.

There are three small chips on the rim. The exterior was coated with a resin, which has darkened the red layer. (Calinescu)

Bibl:
Lowy catalog, pp. 13-14, No. 6
Hendrickx, 2005

5. Black-Topped Deep Bowl
Museum No. 03.007.2000

Height: 3 3/16" (8 cm.) (irregular)
Rim: 5 13/16" (14.6 cm.)
Base: 3" (7.5 cm.)

With evenly balanced proportions of base to height of 1:1, this vessel shows signs of vertical burnishing and lustrous black on the outside, which covers nearly half the exterior. It is closest to B18g in the Corpus.

The interior black surface may be modern, and the exterior seems to have been airbrushed or washed with a diluted stain to improve the tonality. (Calinescu)

Bibl:
Lowy catalog, p. 14, No. 7

6. Black-Topped Deep Bowl
Museum No. 03.008.2000

Height: (irregular) 4 5/8" to 4 3/4" (4 7/8 = 12.3 cm.)
Rim: 5 7/16" (13.8 cm.)
Base (irregular) 2 1/2 to 2 5/8" (2 1/2" = 6.3 cm.)

With proportions of base to height of approximately 1 to 1.75, this is an evenly shaped vessel with numerous irregularities in its dimensions indicating heavy use. It is close to B18k in the Corpus, which Kaiser places in Nagada Ib (1957, pl. 21), a date confirmed by Wilkinson (1996), who records this type among the first two items in his seriation of the Mostagedda cemetery in tomb 1843 (p. 114). It is one of the earliest pots in the cemetery (p. 50) and appears in his group 1, which equates to Nagada Ib. (p. 49) It was horizontally burnished at the top where the black appears as a regular band ranging from 5/8" to one inch. An irregular black spot in the middle of the body was probably made during firing, as were the two small gouges where tempering material in the clay burned out.

The black top may have been over-painted to unify or improve its appearance. There seems to be an overall coating of a resin or varnish on the exterior surface. (Calinescu)

Bibl:
Lowy catalog, p. 14, No. 8

7. Black-Topped Cup
Museum No. 03.009.2000

Height: 3 1/2" (8.9 cm.)
Rim: 3 5/16" (8.4 cm.)
Base: 1 13/16" (4.5 cm.)

When new, this must have been beautiful, with its pleasing shape and color. It has a practical size and shape for eating, fitting easily in one hand and sitting steadily on its sharp-edged base. Petrie (1901) places it on his chart of most common types.

It is moderately well-made with one side at a steeper angle than the other and some rough gouges on the diagonally burnished body. The black areas on the interior and exterior correspond with one another.

This vessel is like B18b in the Corpus, with sequence dates of 33-62, which places it in Nagada I and II as does Payne. She dates the examples in the Ashmolean Museum to IIb and Ib respectively. (p. 36, nos. 130, 131) Hendrickx, 2005, dates it to Ib. (p. 12)

Bibl:
Lowy catalog, pp. 14-15, No. 9
Payne, 1993
Hendrickx, 2005

BLACK-TOPPED BEAKERS

There are four beakers of similar size and shape in the collection, with slender proportions, opening up to their widest point at the rim. They were dinnerware, and can be easily tipped off their bases. All show wear patterns on their narrow bottoms indicating that they would be pushed into the sand for stability during the meal. They were probably used for liquid and would hold a single portion.

All are Nile Silt and have the characteristic color of Black-Topped ware, with what was originally a lustrous black top forming an irregular shape around the top of the vessel, followed by a variety of colors in roughly horizontal bands covering the rest, usually a feathery grayish area followed by a dull orange or red moving to a plum red. Finkenstaedt has called this a "rainbow" coloration. (1981, p. 7)

The interiors of these pots are surprisingly rough, in contrast to the careful treatment of the exteriors. The bottoms appear to have been coil built quickly, often with bumpy surfaces on the sides, as if the coils were roughly smoothed. There are clear signs on the top of the interior of the horizontal turning that was used to form and smooth the rim.

Most have chips and cracks, especially on the rim, and abraded surfaces indicating that they were heavily used.

Date

Nagada I-II c. 3900-3300 BCE

Despite being grouped together in this catalog, their slight differences account for each having a different Corpus number, although all fall within B25, 26, 27, which Patch dates to Ib-IIb, c. 3900-3650 BCE (personal communication). Kaiser, 1957, p. 73 places B26e in level Ic and indicates that B ware is almost exclusively slender beakers with sloping walls. Endesfelder dates B27c, 25L, 25d, 25f, 27g to IIa, (1990, p. 110) and Payne (1993, p. 39, cat. 172) places the Ashmolean example in Ic. Kaiser places B26c in level Ic (1957) and Payne dates a similar pots, including one in the Ashmolean to IIa (1992, p.186; 1993, p. 40, cat. no. 179). Hendrickx has argued that Nagada Ic and IIa are so close as to be considered the same level. (1996, p. 39) B22j dates to IIa-c according to Payne, 1992, pp. 186-187 and IIb-IIc. (1993, p. 38, cat. 151,152) Hendrickx (2005, p. 13) dates most of the B25 and B27 series, what he calls slender beakers, often with modeled rims, to IIb. Wilkinson, 1996, only mentions two of these: B25L (03.003.2000), which he calls a medium-sized tall beaker and B22j (03.005.2000), named a tall narrow beaker. (p. 105)

Coll: Lowy

Bibl:

Petrie, 1921
Kaiser, 1957
Finkenstaedt, 1981
Endesfelder, 1990
Payne, 1992
Payne, 1993
Hendrickx, 1996
Wilkinson, 1996
Hendrickx, 2005

8. Black-Topped Beaker
Museum No. 03.002.2000

Height: 8 1/4" (20.6 cm.)
Rim: 4 3/4" (12.1 cm.)
Rim thickness: 1/8" (.2 cm.)
Base: 1 1/2" (3.5 cm.)

Nagada IIb c. 3700 BCE

This vessel has slim and elegant proportions of 1:5.75 (base to height) and base to rim relationship of 1:3.5.

Much care was lavished on the exterior, where the burnishing is horizontal at the top and vertical on the body. There is great variety of movement and color on the surface, starting with its regular vertical marks. The entire surface coloration is generally irregular, probably due to the way in which it was fired. It is not perfectly symmetrical and the rim seems slightly uneven.

B26f is the closest Corpus example, differing only in a smaller rim. It has the exact base to height proportion as our example but differs in the proportion of base to rim.

Bibl:
Lowy catalog, p. 12, No. 2

9. Black-Topped Beaker
Museum No. 03.003.2000

Height: 8 5/8" (21.8 cm.)
Rim: 4 1/2" (11.3 cm.)
Base (irregular): 2 1/16" (5.2 cm.)

Nagada IIa c. 3800 BCE

This vessel has proportions of base to height of 1:4 and base to rim of 1:2, designed to fit in the hand. Its rough vertical burnishing on the body left grooves and slightly angular marks, as if the pot were shaved. The irregular black top has a horizontal burnish. The bottom may originally have been flat, but as the result of repeated use is now so worn that it leans when resting upright. On the interior there is a faint indication of a spiral at the bottom, where the potting started. The position of the colors is the same on the interior and exterior: black around the first inch on the top although much of it is worn off, then an ochre band, then black result from irregular heat control during firing or staining during burial. (Calinescu)

B25L in the Corpus is closest with the same height and rim diameter. Wilkinson (1996, p. 115) locates this pot type in grave 057 at Mahasna, which appears at the beginning of the second half of his seriation group 1b (p. 52). 1b equates to Nagada Ic-IIa (p. 51), so the most likely date at Mahasna is IIa.

Bibl:
Lowy catalog, p. 13, No. 3

10. Black-Topped Beaker
Museum No. 03.004.2000

Height: 9" (22.6cm.)
Rim: 4 5/16" (10.9 cm.)
Base: 1 3/8" (3.5 cm.)

Nagada Ic-IIa c. 3900-3650 BCE

This carefully made, perfectly symmetrical beaker has the most slender proportions of any of the others in the collection: base to height, 1:6.5, somewhat mitigated by the proportions of base to rim of a bit more than 1:3. The elegant appearance and nearly perfect condition of this piece makes it one of the most beautiful vessels in our collection. Its narrow black band is carried over the lip to cover a small upper edge of the reddish interior.

It is closest to B26c in the Corpus and with nearly the same proportions. Kaiser places it in level Ic (1957) and Payne dates a similar pots to IIa. (1992, p. 186; 1993, p. 40, cat. no. 179) Hendrickx (2005, p. 12) dates B26c to Ic and mentions its explicit concave upper part.

Bibl:
Lowy catalog, p. 13, No. 4

11. Black-Topped Beaker
Museum No. 03.005.2000

Height: 8 1/4" (20.8 cm.)
Rim: 4 5/16" (10.9 cm.)
Base: 1 5/8" (4.1 cm.)

Nagada I c. 3900-3800 BCE

This elegant beaker is the product of skillful potting, with its symmetrical and subtly curving shape. The sides slowly bend up from the bottom and slightly turn in about one-half inch under the rim to form a small neck, then gracefully move out to terminate the form.

A 2 x 5 cm. loss in the rim exposes the black fabric.

B22j in the Corpus is similar, which Payne, 1992, pp. 186-187 dates to IIabc. Wilkinson, 1996, locates this pot type at Mahasna in grave 032 (p. 115), where most of the pots like this are in his seriation category 1a, which equates to Nagada Ia-Ic. (p. 51) The last appearance of this type is at the beginning of his category 1b (p. 52), which is equivalent to Nagada Ic. (p. 51) Hendrickx (2005, p. 12) dates it to Ib.

Bibl:
Lowy catalog, p. 13, No. 5

12. Black-Topped Beaker
Museum No. 03.001.2000

Height: 11-11 1/2" (27.8 – 29.1 cm.) slightly irregular height
Rim: 6 3/16" (15.7 cm.)
Base: 3 5/16" (8.4 cm.)

Nile Silt

Nagada Ib-IIa c.3900-3650 BCE

This is a very common shape in B ware with its finely made lustrous black surface, straight walls and its base to rim proportions of approximately 1:2. It can be found in a wide range of sizes. Its open mouth is the widest part of the vessel, which allows one to easily reach into it with a hand or implement such as a shell or small cup. Its broad base and size suggest it could hold liquid and be used in cooking. Our example must have originally been beautiful, but its damaged and tilting shape show that history has not been kind to it.

The closest Corpus example is B27d. While the B27 series as a whole is consistent in showing rims, the B27d example in the Corpus does not, nor does it indicate the worn, uneven base that causes our pot to lean when it stands. This vessel may originally have been more precisely thrown and just be showing signs of heavy use, or it may originally have been made by a less than perfect potter.

This pot has the characteristic color organization of B ware, with its rich red body and irregular black top that here covers the top fourth of the jar. On the body are the characteristic roughly horizontal sections of color that start with the black top, then move through a feathery transition to a more orange band that is followed by the red that covers most of the pot. The surface shows signs of burnishing that is slightly off the vertical for most of the pot, but clearly diagonal on the black top.

The interior is typical for B ware, probably coil built at the bottom, with most of the vessel slab built. One can see horizontal markings throughout and a progression of color, starting with black, running from the rim to about an inch down the interior, followed by a brownish color, followed by a light ochre that covers the bottom 4 inches of the interior. At the top of the jar, cracks and six sizeable chips reveal that it was fired black all the way through, as opposed to the black being deposited only on the surface. Here is a case where the pot must have been turned top down into a thick mass of organic material that covered both the inside and outside and that remained hot enough to "cook" the pottery all the way through.

The vessel is complete but shows signs of repair where the two big pieces that broke off the pot are clearly visible. There are three small chips in the lower body where some of the larger pieces of tempering material may have burned away during firing.

Date

Petrie gives a sequence date of 31-55 (that is Nagada I-II) for B27d. Kaiser (1957) has shapes similar to this appearing in Levels Ia-Ic and IIa and mentions a B27d pot at Abydos from level Ia (It is a BlackTopped vessel but was colored to look like C ware). (p. 73) He adds that at Abydos in Ib most of the B ware is open form but with curving walls such as 27b (our 27d is a smaller version of this shape). (p. 73) Payne dates it to IIa. (1992, p. 186) Hendrickx dates the B27 series to IIb. (2005, p. 13)

Coll: Lowy

Bibl:
Petrie, 1921
Kaiser, 1957
Lowy catalog, pp. 11-12, No. 1, illustrated.
Payne, 1992
Hendrickx, 2005

13. Black-Topped Beaker
Museum No. 01.006.2003

Height: 18 1/8" (45.2 cm.)
Rim: 9 11/16" (24.5 cm.)
Base: 4 1/2" (11.5 cm.)

Nile Silt

Nagada I c. 3900-3800 BCE

The largest pot in our collection, it seems too big for anything except storage. But most vessels used for such a purpose have a more closed top. It is a striking piece, with a broad, slightly rounded, sharp edged base and a slightly everted simple rim and seems very close to a vase illustrated as one of the commonest types in Petrie (1901). It has a relatively narrow band of black at the top, with the interior completely covered in black. Inside one can see the concentric marks as the thick coils were smoothed, probably with a shell or piece of wood. Its size and near perfect symmetry, with proportions of base to height of 1:4, base to rim of 1:2, reveal the Predynastic potter's control and ability.

This piece has two marks scratched onto its surface, on opposite sides of the jar. Normally such scratched marks are interpreted as "owner's marks," and the two different ones may indicate successive ownership, although there is no way of knowing when such marks were applied and they could be modern. Hess discovered in Petrie (Naqada and Ballas, p. 11) his comment: "Marks were occasionally found on the pots ... they were nearly all scratched on the pots after baking probably by the owners. The usual forms were a cross, a crescent, a palm-tree, a scorpion, a mark like a gallows, and two instances a pentagram." Hess described one mark as a crescent shape, made up of three vertical curved lines, beginning in the red area and moving up to the bottom edge of the black top, and indicated a similar owner's mark in Naqada and Ballas No. 426, although it is shown in the publication upside down. The second mark is hard to interpret. It has two vertical marks topped with a small circle, out of which three angular lines emerge, one to the left and two to the right. On either side of this image are a curve and two diagonal marks, a short one running from upper left to lower right and a longer one from lower left to upper right. There is a vertical scratch further to the right that may be deliberate or may have been made by chance. Interestingly enough both of the similar Ashmolean pots also have incised pot marks. (Payne, 1993, nos. 163, 164) Aside from the idea that the marks indicate ownership, they might also refer to contents, especially for a large storage pot. (Van den Brink, 1992, p. 276, n. 4.)

The lower part of the pot has a fair amount of abrasion, with chips and possible repairs to the top edge, all revealing either a black fabric, or colored to blend in with the black top.

Date

There are many similar shapes in the Petrie Corpus under the numbers 25 and 27, the closest being 25c with a sequence date of 31-41, which Kaiser (1957) illustrates in level Ib. Payne dates two similar pots from Nagada in the Ashmolean Museum to Nagada I. (1993, p. 39, Nos. 163, 164, but in 1992, pp. 186-187 noted dates of Ic and IIc.) Hendrickx, (2005, p. 12) dates B25C to Ib. Wilkinson notes that only one pot of this type appeared in Mostagedda, in grave 1843. (1996, p. 114)

Coll: Harer

Bibl:
Petrie, 1896
Petrie, 1901
Petrie, 1921
Kaiser , 1957
Scott, 1992, cat. No. 3A, pp. 14-15
Van den Brink, 1992
Payne, 1992
Payne, 1993,
Wilkinson, 1996
Hess, Seminar Report, CSUSB, 2004
Hendrickx, 2005

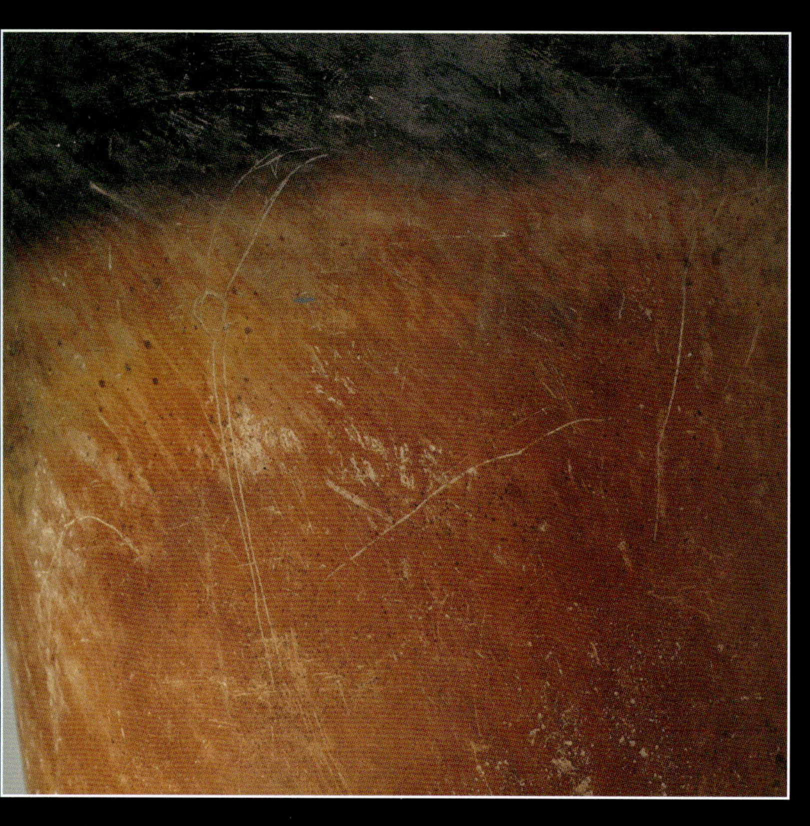

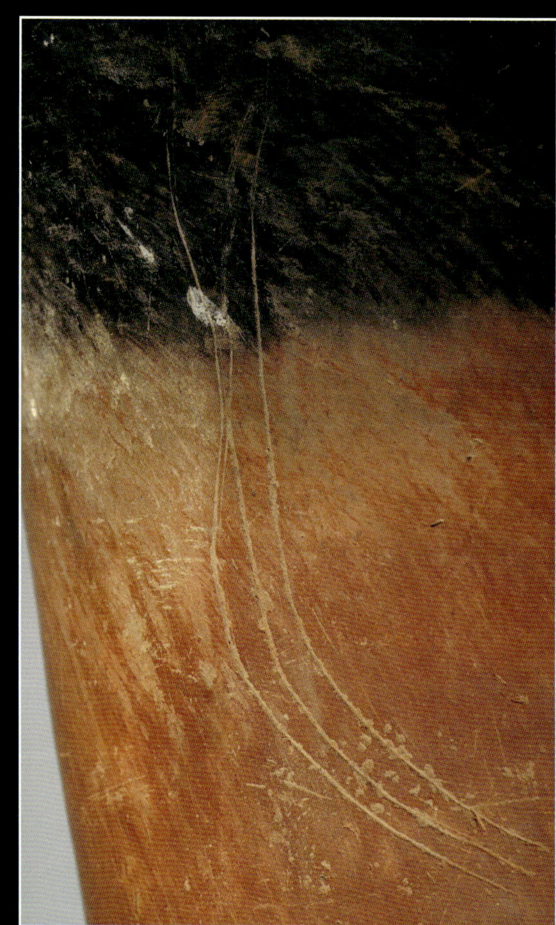

BLACK-TOPPED JARS

Nile Silt

Nagada I-IIc, c.3900-3500 BCE

Four similar slender jars appear in the collection (03.013.2000, 03.016.2000, 01.001.2003, 01.004, 2003). They were a popular and prominent type in a Predynastic dinner service, with their elegant shapes and high-shoulders that fit nicely in the hand, and are appropriate for drinking or serving. The smaller vessels were probably used for wine, the larger ones for beer or milk. Their rims facilitate pouring and their small bases were probably pushed into soft earth when set down. All show signs of vertical or diagonal burnishing on the body and horizontal patterns created at the top both on the exterior and interior, which indicate the smoothing process with a piece of leather or some kind of material used to create this part of the pot. They have the subtle "rainbow" color effects on the exterior characteristic of Black-Topped ware, normally the result of varied temperatures during firing. (Finkenstaedt, Cleveland, 1985, p. 78)

Date

They are similar to Corpus B57b, about which Kaiser (1957) speaks often. He identifies this beaker-like vessel with wide opening and curved edges in the southern section of the Armant cemetery, especially in the northern part of it. This position dates the type to Nagada I and the transition to Nagada II. (pp. 69,70) Endesfelder (1990, p. 110, 112, 113) dates it to Ic-IIc. Patch dates it IIa-IIc. (1991, p. 457 and p. 473, pl. 9) Payne places it in IIa, IIb, and III. (1992, pp. 186-188) Hendrickx notes that it occurs frequently (1996, p. 45) and on p. 65, note 7 says it is one of the types that Kaiser treats inconsistently in text and plates. Wilkinson identifies the type, which he calls a miniature closed jar with convex sides and flat base (p. 105) in specific graves in Matmar, Mahasna and Armant (pp. 112, 113, 115, 116) and their date-range is I-IIc, consistent with that proposed by the authors cited above. At Matmar the graves holding this pot type (3007, 3776, 3081 1093, 3116) appear in his seriation categories 1 to 2b, which equate to Nagada Ib-IIc. (pp. 48-49) At Mahasna, grave 006 (p. 115), is in the last part of his category 1b, which equates to Nagada IIa. (pp. 51-52) At Armant graves 1421, 1472, 1502, 1526 (p.116) appear from the first half of his category 1 to early 2a, which equate to Nagada I-IIb. (pp. 53-54)

Bibl:
Petrie, Corpus
Kaiser, 1957
Endesfelder, 1990
Patch, 1991
Payne, 1992
Wilkinson, 1996
Hendrickx, 1996

14. Black-Topped Jar
Museum No. 03.013. 2000

Height: 7 5/8" (19.2 cm.)
Rim: 3 3/4" (9.5 cm.)
Greatest width: 4 5/8" (11.7 cm.)
Base: 1 1/4" (3.2 cm.)

This jar, with a 1:6 proportion of base to height, is the largest of the group and has a carefully formed thickened rim. The black top is lustrous and covers the top third of the vessel. Under it is a one-inch high dark orange zone that leads to the remaining plum red surface. There is an area of diagonal rippling in the clay surface under the burnishing marks that result from the potting process. The cut base can support the jar.

Inside the pot, Nile Silt fabric forms a flat bottom and the walls reveal horizontal smoothing. Two inches from the top is an indentation, probably created as the potter's fingers shaped the rim, also indicated by fine horizontal lines showing how the hand moved around the top of the pot. The exterior rim looks like its bottom edge was marked with a sharp tool.

A modern coating of lacquer has been applied to the surface that appears glossy and orange-brown in color. A brown-black coating was applied over the black part of the top as well. (Calinescu)

Coll: Lowy

Bibl:
Lowy catalog, p. 17, No. 13

15. Black-Topped Jar
Museum No. 03.016.2000

Height: 5 1/2" (13.9 cm.)
Rim: 3" (7.6 cm.)
Greatest width: 3 1/2" (8.9 cm.)
Base: 5/8" (1.6 cm.)

This well-made vessel has a bulbous but elegant body with a turned and slightly thickened rim. Because of its tiny, almost nonexistent small, flat base, it can only stand on its own if placed carefully on a flat surface, so it was probably set on a stand that applied pressure only at the bottom, which is the only place where wear marks appear. It has proportions of 1:8.6 (base to height) and 1:5.5 (base to greatest width). It appears to have been heavily used and somewhat abraded, with one chip on the rim that reveals its black fabric. Inside the smoothly finished walls are gray, with horizontal marks on the rim. An irregular black top runs 5/8 to 1 3/4 inches down the body, which was once iridescent, letting us imagine the lovely piece of dinnerware this once was.

The rim has been restored with a gray material, which was painted black. (Calinescu)

Coll: Lowy

Bibl:
Lowy catalog, p. 18, No. 16

16. Black-Topped Jar
Museum No. 01.001.2003

Height: 4 3/4" (11.5cm.)
Rim: 2 3/4" (7.1 cm.)
Wall width: 1/8" (.3 cm.)
Greatest width: 3 1/8" (8 cm.)
Base: 7/8" (2.2 cm.)

The smallest example in this group, it was probably used like a modern drinking glass. Its proportions of base to height are 1:5, base to rim, 1:2.25 and base to greatest width, 1:3.5. Its black top is very irregular, ranging from 1/2 to 2 1/4 inches down the side of the vessel. It is well worn, verifying its popularity and use but signs of the lustrous black top and the shiny red body can still be seen. The interior is black on its rim and top where a chip shows the Nile Silt fabric. The lower interior walls and bottom are roughly made in contrast to the thin walls at the top. There is an area of indentations toward the bottom of the pot made before the red surface was polished. This was made during its manufacture when pots rested and dried on thick woven mats, which created this rippled impression.

An overall coating of resin or varnish has been applied to the exterior surface, which minimizes the scratches, abrasion and losses. Black paint was added over the top. (Calinescu)

Coll: Harer

Bibl:
Scott, 1992, cat. No. 2A, p.14

17. Black-Topped Jar
Museum No. 01.004.2003

Height: 5 1/8" (12.5 cm.)
Rim: 1 9/16" (6.5 cm.)
Wall width: 1/8" (.3 cm.)
Greatest width: 3 1/8" (8 cm.)
Base: 1 1/8" (3 cm.)

This elegant pot is thin-walled and symmetrically shaped with balanced proportions (base to height of 1:4 and base to rim of 1:2). It has the size and function of a modern drinking glass and is in excellent condition. The black part of this pot has retained much of its luster, but the red is more matte, with indications of its original shiny appearance. There is a definite sense of movement and pattern created by the burnishing marks and color organization. This example clearly shows the color fields, running from top to bottom, from a black top, with a wide gray area underneath, followed by roughly horizontal areas of dull orange, reddish-brown and plum-red. A chip on the rim reveals that the black color permeates the entire clay body, a feature of all of this B ware. (Friedman, 1994 p. 350) Hess described the inside as very smooth and indicates a manufacturing line visible on the interior.

The bottom of the jar has deeply gouged paired crossed lines, a common pot mark (Payne, 1993, Fig. 43, no. 870, fig. 44, No. 875) Most of the marks are quite simple, a single or few lines, making up the most elementary of designs. Because the mark is so deep and because it is on the bottom of the jar, it seems likely that this is the potter's mark. Hess found a similar mark in Petrie's Naqada and Ballas, Nos. 156, 161 and 163.

Coll.: Harer

Bibl:
Petrie, 1896
Finkenstaedt, Cleveland, 1985
Scott, 1992, cat. No. 2D, p. 14
Friedman, 1994
Hess, Seminar Report, CSUSB, 2004

18. Black-Topped Jar with Thickened Rim
Museum No. 03.011.2000

Height: 9 13/16 (24.8 cm.)
Rim: 3 3/16" (8.1 cm.)
Greatest width: 5 5/8" (14.3. cm.)
Base: 1 7/8" (4.8 cm.)

Nile Silt

Nagada IIc-IId2 c. 3650-3300 BCE

At nearly ten inches tall, this jar was used for serving purposes, and its shape suggests it held liquid ingredients, because the enclosed top prevents spillage and its rolled rim facilitates pouring. Though much worn, it was originally a spectacular example of Predynastic ware: finely crafted, symmetrical, elegant with its 1:5 proportion of base to height and beautifully decorated, probably used for the beer and wine that were the preferred drinks of fine dining in ancient Egypt. Though it can stand alone, the narrowness of the bottom indicates that for support it would have to rest on a stand or be pushed into soft, sandy earth in order not to topple over, as the worn bottom indicates. There are still some remnants of its luminescent black top and shiny red body, with its vertical burnishing and horizontal rubbing marks around the neck. The black is applied so regularly that it looks like it was painted on. Inside the neck is a reddish color, while the rest of the interior is ochre. There is a circular indentation on the interior of the pot's wall as it begins to rise from the base and an inch above that is a circular linear indentation around the pot that appears to have been made by the potter's fingers. The interior surface has circular horizontal markings on its entire surface. A ridge going around the top of the interior indicates where the potter's fingers pressed as he grasped the wall of the pot to form the neck.

Its shape is virtually perfect but it has an eroded surface and is marred by some thin cracks and signs of use.

Date

The match in the Corpus for this jar, with its bulbous shape, fairly enclosed top, small flat, clearly-cut bottom, and thickened rim is P40e, which Wilkinson calls a barrel-shaped jar. (p. 105) Since the Black-Topped and Polished Red wares are made of the same fabric and fired the same way (the Black-Topped made different by going through an additional reducing phase) it is appropriate to look for its shape in Petrie's Corpus under both ware categories. Kaiser (1957, p. 70) mentions this pot as appearing in the north section of Armant cemetery, thus transitional between Nagada II and III, and that it is a small version of a barrel-shaped type that is found only in the middle section of the cemetery. He also says that the entire P40 group is a new type of barrel-shaped vessel in IIc, and that it represents a declining quality of surface finish that seems characteristic of the beginnings of IIc to the end of IId and earliest III. (p. 72). He adds that this is one of the clay vessels that appear numerous times in IId. (p. 72) Patch (1991, p. 483, p. 497, pl. 21) dates this type to IIc-IId2. Payne places it in IIc, IIc1 and III. (1992, pp. 187-188) Hendrickx sees it as one of the types during the transition between IId2 and IIIa1. (1996, p. 41) Wilkinson (1996) identifies this type in the cemeteries of Mahasna, Armant and Hierakonpolis (pp. 115-118) where its date conforms to the previous experts, from IIc to IId1. The Mahasna graves 086, 133 both appear at the end of his category 2b (pl. 50), which equates to Nagada IId2 (p. 51); at Armant graves 1446, 1565, 1566 range from the middle of his category 2a to the beginning of 2b (p 54), which equate to Nagada IIc (p. 53); Hierakonpolis graves 066, 087 are respectively the end and middle of his category 1 (p. 57), which equates to IIc-IId1 (p. 56).

Coll: Lowy

Bibl:
Petrie, 1921
Kaiser, 1957
Lowy catalog, pp. 15-16, No. 11
Patch, 1991
Payne, 1992
Hendrickx, 1996
Wilkinson, 1996
Hess, Seminar Report, CSUSB, 2004

19. Black-Topped Jar with slightly Thickened Rim
Museum No. 03.014.2000

Height: 5 1/4" (13.3 cm.)
Rim: 4 3/8" (11 cm.)
Greatest width: 4 13/16" (12.1 cm.)
Base: 1 5/8" (4.1 cm.)

Nile Silt

Nagada IIa-IIc c.3800-3500 BCE

This is a characteristic example of functional tableware and when it was new it must have been appealing with its rounded shape and pretty colors. Its bulbous symmetrical body and slightly thickened, tool-marked rim combined with squat proportions (base to height and base to rim respectively of 1:3 and 1:2.5) makes it fit easily in two hands. It is shorter and squatter than similar examples in the collection and can rest on its own bottom. These characteristics suggest its use as a drinking vessel, like a large beer stein of today, or for serving a liquid. Such use may explain the wear on the bottom part of the vessel. It must have been striking when it was new because there are still signs of lustrous black and red on the pot. The irregular black top ranges from one-fourth to one and one-half inches from the rim, with signs of vertical burnishing on the body, the horizontal polishing appearing only at the rim. Its red body was fired irregularly; some parts are plum and some more orange. This vessel reveals that at one time its interior was black. This could be a stain of some sort left by its contents, or soot from its firing. One can see the Nile Silt clay at the bottom. There is a five-eights inch layer of thicker clay used to form the top and rim, and some evidence of horizontal smoothing by the potter's fingers. The interior is rough. Part of the interior surface popped off (spalling), so there are only remnants of the original surface, mainly on the rim. This damage may be due to use, caustic contents or post-burial salts. (Patch, personal communication) The exterior, much worn today, has one small chip on the rim and two small gouges on the body.

It is possible that an overall clear resin coating was applied in order to consolidate the exterior surface. (Calinescu)

Date

It is close to B72a in the Corpus. Kaiser (1957, p. 69) mentions that this type of more closed-mouth beaker is most numerous in the northern part of the southern section of the cemetery at Armant, but is also recorded in the middle part of the southern section as well. This placement dates the vessel to Nagada I and the turn to Nagada II. Patch (1991, pp. 455, 471) dates it to IIa – b. Payne dates it to IIa,IIb,IId1. (1992, pp. 186-188) Wilkinson calls it a miniature closed jar with convex sides and flat base (p. 105) and finds it very early in the pottery sequence at Mostagedda and Armant. (pp. 50, 54) The pot-type appears in Mostagedda grave 1764 (p. 114), half-way through his seriation category 1, which equates to Ib-Ic-IIa (pp. 49-50). At Armant graves 1473, 1488 it is three quarters of the way through his seriation category 2a, which equates to Nagada IIb-IIc (pp. 53-54).

Coll: Lowy

Bibl:
Petrie, 1921
Kaiser, 1957
Lowy catalog, p. 17, No. 14
Patch, 1991
Payne, 1992
Wilkinson, 1996

20. Black-Topped Jar With Slightly Thickened Rim
Museum No. 03.015.2000

Height: 5 3/8" (13.6 cm.)
Rim: 3 3/4" (9.4 cm..)
Greatest width: 3 13/16" (9.6 cm.)
Base: 1 1/8" (2.8 cm.)

Nile Silt

Nagada IIa-IIb c.3800-3650 BCE

An attractive vessel when new, this jar is carefully made and has a sleek shape formed by a regular parabolic curve subtly altered at the top. It has an irregular, luminous narrow black top and a much worn shiny red surface, vertically burnished except for horizontal marks on the rim. It is precisely balanced so it stands straight even though its flat base is quite worn. On the interior is a smooth base that looks molded while most of the walls show signs of horizontal potting. Black covers the upper rim, followed by up to two inches of gray, leading to the brown Nile Silt interior.

What is most striking about this vase is the carved or impressed mark on its side, made before it was slipped and fired. In this it is similar to the Corpus pot, which also has a pot mark, although it is not the same shape and Petrie does not indicate if it was under the slip or scratched into it. Such marks often appear on Predynastic pots and most experts agree that the impressed marks under the slip/wash and burnishing, such as this one, are "potter's marks" (they identify the potter) and marks scratched into the pot after it is finished are "owner's marks." This pot is so fine that one can see why the potter would have wanted to mark it. Based on Dynastic practice, it could also be a label, identifying the vessel's contents. (Van den Brink, 1992, p. 276, n. 4). It could be a bent arm, but the Lowy catalog suggests that this mark "appears to be the representation of the foreleg of a cow. This is the same type found on later tomb reliefs and temple offering scenes showing cattle being slaughtered and the front right foreleg being offered up in sacrifice." (pp. 17-18) These marks are tantalizing because they are the first indications of written language. They could be a sign of pride of craft or ownership or an early example of the need to inventory goods. The sign could also relate to the pot's function, perhaps used during some funerary practice such as a commemorative meal, or as an offering vessel in a religious ceremony. The pot is damaged in several places: scratches on the body, three chips on the rim and an abraded surface

Date

This is another piece of tableware whose closest parallel in the Corpus is B72b, with which it shares similar proportions (base to height is 1:5, and base to rim is 1:3). Petrie's sequence date of 35-51 (Nagada Ib – IIc) needs some revision. While Kaiser (1957, pp. 69-70) does not mention this specific vessel, he places B72a and B72c – all similar shapes – in Nagada I and the beginnings of Nagada II. Hendrickx argued against making distinctions in Nagada I. (1996, p. 39) Patch suggests a IIa-IIc date range (1991, pp. 457, 573, pl. 9), which encompasses the IIa and IIb dates proposed respectively by Payne (1992, pp. 186-187), and in the Ashmolean Museum catalog. (1993, No. 278, p. 47) Wilkinson (1996), who calls this type a miniature squat beaker (p. 105), locates an example at Matmar (grave 3082) (p. 113) early in his seriation category I, which equates to Nagada Ib-Ic-IIa (pp. 49-50). At Mahasna this pot-type is in grave 053 (p.115) about one third of the way into his seriation category 1b, which equates to Nagada Ic-IIa (pp. 51-52).

Coll: Lowy

Bibl:
Petrie, 1921
Kaiser, 1957
Lowy catalog, pp. 16, 17, No. 15
Patch, 1991
Van den Brink, 1992
Payne, 1992
Payne, 1993
Wilkinson, 1996

BLACK-TOPPED JARS WITH SMALL OR POINTED BASES

Nile Silt

Nagada IIa-IId2 c.3800-3300 BCE

Vessels of this shape were important and influential and appear often in Predynastic Egyptian ceramics. Petrie identified them as among the most common types (1901). Elongated and elegant, their bases are so small they cannot stand alone and need a support, or they need to be pushed into a relatively soft surface, such as sandy earth. The shape must have had practical advantages (probably for storage) and perhaps aesthetic appeal as well. Our three examples have vertical burnishing on the body and horizontal burnishing on the top, characteristic of this ware, with signs of their iridescent black coating and shiny red surface. The experts assume that the best ware is that which is finely and highly polished (in which no marks show) and the lesser quality ware shows its burnishing marks. But there may have been aesthetic concerns in the visible burnishing because of the rhythms created. They are excellent examples of the purity of form and precision of potting so characteristic of the Black-Topped ware and always impressive for hand-built pieces.

Bibl:
Petrie, 1901
Petrie, 1921
Kaiser, 1957
Patch, 1991
Payne, 1992
Payne, 1993
Wilkinson, 1996
Hendrickx, 2005

21. Black-Topped Jar With Thickened Rim
Museum No. 03.010.2000

Height: 15 13/16" (38.4 cm.)
Rim: 6 3/16" (15.6 cm.)
Greatest width: 7" (17.7 cm.)
Base: 1 3⁄4" (4.4 cm.)

One of the two largest pots in the collection and in poor condition now, it was originally a symmetrically formed and dramatically colored high-shouldered jar. Its tall, slender, balanced appearance is due to its proportions of base to height of 1:9 and width to height of 1:2. It sits on a small flat base with fairly crisp edges. The irregular black top comes down about one-third of the way on the exterior and 1 3⁄4 inches from the top on the interior, where it is followed by a three inch deep gray area; the rest of the interior is brown. There are signs of paddling to thin and shape the walls that left a series of vertical marks on the interior and a horizontal break suggests finely made coil construction. The interior bottom is flat in only a small area, then the walls begin to rise, showing signs of their horizontal smoothing of the combined coil and slab construction.

This pot provides a good example of a thickened rim, created by moving it around on a surface, such as a straw mat or a piece of wood, and holding the hand steady on the top edge of the jar as it is turned. A close look reveals the small horizontal ridges created by this process.

This vessel shows signs of rough treatment, which is to be expected from a pot whose size and open mouth provided easy access for storage. Of course, rougher and less expensive ware was appropriate for storage as well, but Friedman suggested that some polished Black-Topped pots larger than this were used in beer manufacturing. (1994, p. 672)

Large parts covering an area 4 1⁄4 inches high and 11 inches wide broke off the pot and have been put back on. There are chips on the rim and surface, along with gouges, some made when parts of the tempering agent burned out while firing.

On the upper part of the pot, surface loss has been over-painted black to disguise repairs. (Calinescu)

Date

Hess gives B53a as its Corpus number. Petrie's sequence dates for this item are 38-66, which covers all of Nagada II, and Kaiser draws a similar conclusion (see discussion in entry 01.007.2003), finding similar examples in Levels IIb-IId2 as does Patch. (1991, pp. 458, 478, pl. 14)

This is the only pot in our collection to appear often in Kaiser's classification of Predynastic ceramics (1957), and he has much to say about it. He identifies it as one of a group of B vessels that are only found in the middle part of the southern section of the Armant cemetery. (p. 70) Since he established that the cemetery (which begins in Nagada II) starts in the south and spreads to the north, this makes B53a one of the earliest pot types. He describes it as a new form that first appears in IIa, but whose full development is in IIb and later. (p. 71) This shape was so useful and/or beautiful that it appears in other wares as well. Kaiser says it is similar to B ware found in IIa, such as 53a, 58b (p. 72) [which is in Petrie's 1901 chart of most common types], and is an example of the closed forms that characterize B ware in Nagada IIb and IIc. (p. 71) It is also one of the few B ware shapes that corresponds to R ware. (p. 71) Kaiser sees this vase as a source for a new kind of barrel-shape vessel in P ware that develops in IIc and later (p. 72) and in Nagada IIc, was an influence on B50 – a new kind of pointed-bottomed vessel. (p. 72)

Perhaps because of Kaiser's extensive comments, Hendrickx noted that it is one of the examples where Kaiser gives different information about the pot in the text and in the plates. (1996, p. 43, n. 7) In fact, Hendrickx (p. 43) says that Kaiser never intended the plates to be absolute guidelines, but rather an "idealized outline of the development of the stufen (levels)." Scholarly opinion is unanimous about the Nagada II date for this type of pot. Endesfelder, discussing Armant pots, dates the one in grave 1466 to IIa, those in graves 1553, 1556, IIc and those in graves 1511, 1521 to IId. (1990, p. 90) Payne dates similar pots to IIb, IIc, IId1 (1992, pp. 187-188) and the next year placed the three Nagada examples in the Ashmolean Museum in IIbc (1993, p. 43, Nos. 223-225) and then dates the same shape in chaff-ware to IIc and IId1. (1993, p. 94, cat. Nos. 778, 779)

Wilkinson (1996) is in substantial agreement with this dating, although his study of the Armant material differs slightly from Endesfelder (he puts grave 1466 in IIb and 1521 in IIc) and he finds the pot-type appearing earlier at Matmar than at the other sites. What Wilkinson calls a large closed tapering jar with pronounced rim (p. 105) is a very popular jar. It appears in five of the six sites he studied. It appears in six graves at Marmar (3007, 3130, 3132, 5105, 5116, 5117) (p. 112) which are in his seriation groups 1 to early 2b, which equate to Nagada Ib-IId1. (pp. 49-50) Seven graves at Armant contain this type: 1466, 1499, 1511, 1521, 1553, 1565, 1566 (pp. 116-117), which are in the seriation sequences 2a-2b, equating to Nagada IIb-IIIa1. (pp. 52-53) At Mostagedda, grave 1613 (p 114) is early in his sequence category 2, which equates to Nagada IIb-IIc. (pp. 49-50) At Mahasna,

graves 083, 086 (p. 115) are in the last part of his seriation sequence 2a, which equates to Nagada IIb. (pp. 50-51) To summarize, Wilkinson finds this type in Matmar and Mostagedda in IIb, at Armant from IIb to IId2 and at Matmar from Ib to IIc, which demonstrates that rather than Predynastic Egypt being a monolithic culture, different sites developed similar ceramics at different times.

Hendrickx notes the new occurrence in IIa of large, flat-based regularly curved jars with strongly marked rims (2005, p. 13) while in IIc Black-Topped pottery is dominated by shouldered jars with a small base and modeled rim. (pl. 14)

Coll: Lowy

Bibl:

Lowy catalog, p. 15, No. 10.
Endesfelder, 1990
Friedman, 1994
Hendrickx, 1996
Brooke Hess, Seminar Paper, CSUSB, 2004

22. Black-Topped Jar
Museum No. 01.005.2003

Height: 9 3/4" (24 cm.)
Rim: 3 1/4" (8.2 cm)
Lip: 1/4" thick (.7 cm.)
Greatest width: 4 1/16" (10.5 cm.)
Base: 1/2" (1.2 cm.)

This pot has an elegant shape with an even thickened rim, which is a classic form in Polished Red ware, with proportions of base to height of 1:19.5 and base to rim of 1:6.5. The piece is in relatively good condition with a surface color that moves from black at the top through orange to red at the bottom. The asymmetrical black area covers only the part of the jar above the shoulder. The entire interior has a black coating on it. It may be a storage piece, but because it is relatively small size, it is more likely used for serving at a meal. Due to its clear, strong and prominent thickened rim, facilitating pouring, it probably held a liquid.

The nicely repaired pot was originally broken. One can see the three big pieces from the interior. One piece makes up the top one third of the jar and about one half the circumference and there is a long vertical crack.

Date

B39a in the Corpus is exactly the same size as this piece, and Petrie gave it sequence dates of 44-61, fully in Nagada II and the beginning of Nagada III. Kaiser places such slender, pointed vessels only in Nagada IIc, which is two levels (stufen) before the beginning of Nagada III. (1957, p. 72) But Hendrickx argues that late Nagada II and early Nagada III are so close in time that the finer distinctions that are made in pottery studies are probably illusory. (1996, p. 41) Patch, who dates this jar type to IIc-IId2, (1991, pp. 458, 477, pl. 13) and Payne to IId1 agree to a date range in the late Predynastic. (1992, p. 188) (1993, pl. 42, cat. No. 211) Hendrickx says that Black-Topped pottery is IIc and is dominated by shouldered jars with a small base and a modeled rim and similar shapes with a pointed base like this one. (2005, p. 14) He adds that in IId1 this type is among the regularly curved and shouldered jars with modeled rims that mark the rare occurrence of B ware at this time (p. 15).

Coll: Harer

Bibl:
Scott, 1992, cat. No. 2E, p. 14
Hendrickx, 1996

23. Black-Topped Jar
Museum No. 01.007.2003

Height: 14" (35 cm.)
Rim: 6 5/16" (16.1 cm.)
Width: 7 1/4" (18.4 cm.)
Base: 1 1/2" (3.8 cm.)

This jar has proportions of base to height of 1:9, base to width of 1:5 and width to height of 1:2. It was probably used for storage, being too big for serving at any meal other than a banquet. It has a well-made rolled rim, short neck and a worn flat bottom. The soft demarcation between the black area at the top and the lower light red leading to the darker red that covers most of the body provides a counterpoint to the precision of the contours. It is exactly the harmony resulting from such contradictory elements that makes the best Black-Topped ware so fascinating. On the interior this piece has a black rim about one inch deep, with a brownish color of Nile silt covering the rest of the vessel.

Three major vertical cracks reveal the places where slabs were joined together, making up the upper two-thirds of the vessel, above the coil-made base. There is one large modern chip replacement.

Date

This jar appears throughout the chronological periods according to Petrie, and in most of Nagada II, according to Kaiser (1957). It is closest to Corpus B53b, with a sequence date of 33-75. Kaiser (1957, p. 70-71) says it first appears in IIa with full development in IIb but he charts it in IId1, not the first time that what he says about a pot in his text differs from what he puts in his chart. While Endesfelder, 1990, puts a similar pot from Armant (grave 1472) in Nagada IIa, most other studies place it in late Nagada II. Patch dates it to IIb-IId2. (1991, pp. 458, 478, pl. 14) Payne dates similar material to IIc, IId1 (1992, pp. 187-188) and in 1993 dates the Nagada pots of this shape in the Ashmolean museum to IIb and IId1 respectively. (pp. 43,44, Nos. 226, 227) Wilkinson (1996), who calls this pot-type a large closed tapering jar with pronounced rim (p. 105), finds it at Matmar, Armant and Mahasna. In Matmar, graves 3077, 3130 (p. 113) are respectively the first grave with this type in seriation group 1 and the next to the last in group 2b, which equate respectively to Nagada Ib and IIc (pp. 48-49). At Armant grave 1566 (p. 117), it is mid-way in the seriation sequence 2a, which equates to Nagada IIb-IIc (pp. 53-54) and at Mahasna, grave 080 (p. 115) it is in the last third of his seriation sequence 2b, which equates to IId2 (pp. 51-52). Hendrickx says this type first occurs in IIa but is dominant in IIc. (2005, pp. 13-14). See his comments in the entry for 03.010.2000 above.

Coll: Harer

Bibl:
Endesfelder, 1990
Scott, 1992, cat. No. 3B, pp. 15-17

24. *Black Double Jar
Museum No. EI 02.004.2004

(Pot viewed from less damaged side)

	Left		Right
Height:	2 7/8" (6.9 cm.)		2 15/1 6" (7.1 cm.)
Rim:	1 5/8" (4 cm.)		1" (2.5 cm.)
Width:	2 1/4" (5.5 cm.)		2" (5 cm.)
Base:	5/8" (1.5 cm.)		11/16" (1.7 cm.)
Lugs:	1/2" wide (1.2 cm.)		9/16" wide (1.4 cm.)
	9/16" below rim (1.4 cm.)		3/8" below rim (1 cm.)

Nile Silt

Nagada IIc-IId1 c.3650-3300 BCE

This little pot is one of the rare all black vessels that Petrie called Fancy ware. (Rizkana and Seeher, 1987, p. 66) Its shape, made up of two similar ones joined together, represents a characteristic type of Predynastic vessel. Petrie illustrates the type in Fancy and Decorated Ware. (1921, pls. XVII, XXXI) Needler illustrates one in White Cross-lined ware (1984, p. 178, No. 18) while Payne shows an example in Polished Red ware (1993, p. 180, illustration p. 178, No. 18) and others in Decorated ware. (1993, p. 93, Fig. 37, Nos. 829, 830)

Joining two jars together must signify a specific purpose, such as use in a ceremony. We know that vessel amulets were produced in the Predynastic (Patch, personal communication), and some of the twin pots look like testicles or goat udders, suggesting a connection to the idea of fertility. (Wilkinson, 2003, p. 98) It seems made to be held because the two sides of this pot are attached at the middle at a slight angle that prevents the vessel from standing on its own. The lug handles are not balanced, and one is not pierced all the way through, so this vessel could not be hung either.

The two bowls do not connect on the inside (although some of the Predynastic twin vessels do), so the contents of these two jars were not meant to be mixed while contained in the vessel, but were necessary to appear together. Later, in pharaonic times, figures made offerings in pairs, holding a vessel in each hand. The Dynastic Egyptian mindset was based on polarities of geography (Lower and Upper Egypt), experience (day/night; wet river/dry desert) so it is reasonable to assume similar beliefs in the Predynastic, which might account for the various "twin" pots such as this one.

This pot has experienced rough wear with major damage on one side near the top and lots of nicks and abrasions on the surface.

Date

Similar to F44, SD 50 in the Corpus, which Patch dates to IIc-IId1 (personal communication), except that our pots form a more acute angle, and D33b which is IId1 (Patch, personal communication). Payne, 1992, p. 188 dates F44 to IId1.

Coll: Harer

Bibl:
Petrie, 1921
Rizkana and Seeher, 1987
Payne, 1992
Payne, 1993

P (POLISHED RED WARE)

All early Predynastic pottery is made from Nile Silt, which fires brown or red, so in this sense almost all of it is Polished Red ware. When it is found with painted designs, it is White Cross-Lined ware (C); during the "firing" process the oxygen supply can be cut off, turning the red ware black, creating Black-Topped (B) ware. The largest amount of early polished ware was (P) (Patch, personal communication), but there were always excellent pieces of the rarer Black-Topped and solid black ware, the latter called Fancy (F) ware by Petrie and B-P ware by Federn (Needler, 1981, p. 70). As Petrie studied the huge cemeteries at Nagada, he found the Polished Red appearing slightly later than the Black-Topped ware.

Red ware can be produced in several ways and there is some disagreement about how it is made. Most experts say that simply firing and burnishing the Nile Silt produced the red ware. They think that it was fired in an open bonfire. Only later were kilns developed, and approximately eighteen have been found around Hierakonpolis. (Geller, 1989, p. 41, and n. 4) It is clear that Predynastic potters often added a red wash or slip over the vessel before firing. Friedman says that wash in always thin and translucent, not hiding irregularities in the surface, whereas slip is thicker. (1994, p. 188) Once the pot is burnished or polished, it is impossible to tell what the potter had done in terms of color treatment of the surface.

Most of this pottery was made for domestic use, but the very best pieces seem to have been intended exclusively for the tomb.

POLISHED RED OPEN BOWLS

Two similar bowls in the collection are excellent examples of functional eating vessels. Though varying in size, they are among the most common container types for dining. Both are heavily nicked, chipped and scraped from heavy use. As practical bowls, they must have been produced quickly and in great number and are probably coil made.

Both reveal the burnishing marks that often appear on Predynastic pottery. These usually appear on the outside of vessels, but for open shapes, also appear on the interior. These marks sometimes are horizontal near the rim, but can also be angular, following the direction of the hand-turning and indicating how the vessel was shaped.

Both are close to P1a in the Corpus, Nagada I-IIb, c. 3900-3650 BCE which Patch dates to IIb-IId1 (personal communication). Payne dates it to Ic, IIa (1992, p. 186), while Hendrickx indicates that it appears in both Ia and Ib, arguing that these two dates are the same time period, an argument he also applies to Ic and IIa. (1996, p. 41) In 2005 (p. 12) he placed it in Ib.

Nile Silt

Nagada I   c.3900-3800 BCE

Coll: Lowy

Bibl:
Petrie, 1921
Kaiser, 1957
Payne, 1992
Hendrickx, 1996
Hendrickx, 2005

25. Polished Red Open Bowl
Museum No. 03.017.2000

Height: (irregular) 2 1/4-2 5/8" (5.6-6.5 cm.)
Rim: 6 7/16" (16 cm.)
Base: 2 1/8" (5.4 cm.)

The largest of the two similar Polished Red ware bowls in the collection is suitable for eating soups or stews, about the size of a modern day soup bowl or small serving bowl, with proportion of height to rim of 1:3. Trippel notes what appear to be small nicks inside, which are probably the result of using a shell to scoop out the contents, (Midant-Reynes, 1996, p. 95) while Calinescu thinks they are impressions of fine straw temper, which was burned off during firing. There are chips on the rim and at the top of the exterior, an uneven lip with a one-half-inch crack on the edge and two deep chips close to each other on the surface. The flat bottom and the entire exterior are roughly made, with a slightly bumpy finish with clear signs of vertical, horizontal and angular burnishing inside and outside. There are also some black marks that may be stains or random black strokes on the interior. It is well-balanced and can sit on a flat surface.

There is an overall brush-applied coating of resin or varnish on both interior and exterior surfaces that has darkened with age. (Calinescu)

Bibl:
Lowy catalog, p. 19, No. 17
Payne, 1993
Midant-Reynes, 1996
Mona Trippel, Seminar Report, CSUSB, 2004

26. Polished Red Open Bowl
Museum No. Museum No. 03.018.2003

Height: (irregular) 1 1/2 to 1 3/4" (3.7 – 4.4 cm.)
Rim: 5 1/2" (13.9 cm.)

About the size of a modern day small dessert dish, it has an abraded inner surface with chips off the rim and on the underside, which reveals the Nile Silt fabric. Even so one can see the horizontal smoothing around the rim. This bowl is one of the clearest and most interesting examples of burnishing patterns on its top and bottom, which seem the result of an aesthetic decision. They create an angular rhythm that activates both the interior and exterior of the bowl, not unrelated to the geometric patterns found on the C (White Cross-Lined) ware.

One small deeper loss in the outer edge of the rim appears to be old, as it has burial dirt deposited on it. (Calinescu)

Bibl:
Lowy catalog, p. 19, No. 18

27. Polished Red Open Bowl
Museum No. 03.020.2000

Height: (irregular) 1 1/2 x 1 3/4" (3.7 – 4.2 cm.)
Rim: 4 1/8" (10.5 cm.)
Base: 1 3/4" (4.4 cm.)

Nile Silt

Nagada I-II c.3900-3300 BCE

The smallest of our Polished Red bowls, crisply shaped with a fairly large, cut, flat bottom and angular sides, was clearly intended for table service, probably as a scoop. This is such a practical shape that it had a very long life in Predynastic Egypt.

This piece was over-fired, which is why it was burned black in places. It has a crack in the rim and a number of chips that reveal the black color. There is an ochre-colored concretion (a limestone and calcium deposit resulting from burial) on the exterior and interior and through it one can see a brownish-red color. Despite the extensive use of this bowl (it has lost more than half of its original surface) and various deposits on its surface, the visual evidence reveals that is was originally a Polished Red bowl.

Date

It is very similar in shape to B11k, sequence date 38, except this Corpus example has a larger diameter. Petrie places the vessel at the turn between Nagada I and II. It is also close to P11g that Kaiser cites as an example of a new kind of P ware that appears in IIb, with perfected straight sides and base with some curve at the edge. (1957, p. 71) More recent work suggests a broader date range covering most of Nagada II. Patch dates 11g, described as having flaring sides and a plain, sloping rim, to IIa-IIc. (1991, pp. 480, 493, pl. 17) Payne suggests IIa, IIb, IId1. (1992, pp. 186-188) Hendrickx dates this type to Ic-IId2. (Patch, personal communication)

Coll: Lowy

Bibl:
Petrie, Corpus, 1921
Kaiser, 1957
Lowy catalog, p. 20, No. 20
Patch, 1991
Payne, 1992

28. Polished Red Squat Jar
Museum No. 03.025.2000

Height: (irregular) 3 1/2 - 3 3/4" (8.8 – 9.4cm.)
Rim: 2 3/4" (7 cm.)
Greatest width: 4 1/2" (11.3 cm.)
Lug to lug: 4 3/4" (11.9 cm.)
Wall thickness: 3/16" (.2 cm.)
Lug 1: 1 3/16" (3.2 cm.) at top; 3/4" (1.8 cm.) from rim
Lug 2: 1 1/4" (3.1 cm.) at top; 5/8" (.8 cm.) from rim

Nile Silt

Nagada IIb-IId2 c.3650-3300 BCE

Small bulbous jars in clay and stone were popular and numerous throughout the Predynastic period. This symmetrical, globular necked vessel has a thickened, irregular rim, more turned out on one side than the other. There is a groove on the inside, probably made by the potter's finger, corresponding to the upper level of the exterior lug, indicating where the hand held the vessel to make the neck and rim. It is unpolished with a thin red wash that allows the irregularities of the surface to be seen through it. The red is fairly dark with a few areas lighter in color. The mouth is small enough that one would have to use an implement like a small ivory spoon to get at its contents, or if the contents were liquid enough, one could just tip the vessel and pour them out. The pot fits easily in either one or two hands. It is well-balanced and can sit on a surface, but its round bottom and lugs mean that it was designed to be hung. It probably held something precious, like cosmetic oils or ointments, perhaps perfumed, that had protective and symbolic meaning (Hendrickx, 2004, p. 6) and may have been used for ritualistic and medicinal rather than cosmetic purposes – although the early Egyptians may have not made these kind of distinctions.

The vessel must have been functional because it looks heavily used with an abraded surface. The rim is complete and shows signs of wear (chips and small gouges). There are also cracks in the bottom (both on the interior and exterior) and pits on the surface.

There was an unevenly applied coating on the exterior, which was probably meant to act as a consolidant and/or to unify the surface appearance. (Calinescu)

Date

Close to P80s in the Corpus, but slightly taller with a bit smaller mouth. Although Kaiser says that this shape was initiated in D ware in IIb (1957, p. 71), he indicates that polished red P80k, a similar but squatter version of our pot, is a replica of a stone vessel in Ia. (p. 73) Engelbach shows two F (black polished) pots of this shape, one a bit smaller and one a bit larger. (1923, pl. XXVI) While Endesfelder broadens the date a bit for pots found in two Armant graves, 1440 dated IIb and 1535 dated IIc, (1990, p. 111), Payne suggests IIb. (1992, p. 187)(1993, p. 71, cat. No. 520) . Patch suggests that all the 80s, p, and k vessels date to IIb – IId. (personal communication)

Coll: Lowy

Bibl:
Petrie, 1921
Engelbach, 1923
Kaiser, 1957
Lowy catalog, pp. 22-23, No. 25
Endesfelder, 1990
Payne, 1992
Payne, 1993

29. Polished Red Jar
Museum No. 03.012.2000

Height: 10" (26 cm.)
Rim: 4" (10 cm.)
Greatest width: 7" (18 cm.)
Base: 2 1/4" (6 cm.)

Nile Silt

Nagada IIc-IId2 c. 3650-3300 BCE

This is a nicely shaped but rather crudely finished, barely polished storage jar, probably intended for a special purpose. There was plenty of rough ware for normal storage and transport so perhaps this jar was meant to hold something precious, valuable, or symbolic, used by an important person or for an important ritual.

A large, finely proportioned short-necked jar, its beauty reveals how highly skilled the Predynastic potters were. They hand-built a pot that looks like it was "machined" – it is perfectly symmetrical and elegant in its profiles, balanced and regular, and the same proportions are preserved even when the pot varies in size. It is so beautiful that we are not surprised to find it in the chart of the most common types. (Petrie, 1901)

The relationship of base to height is c. 1:4.3, base to greatest width 1:3 and base to mouth 1:1.6. The overall effect is of a fairly tall, very regular elongated globular vessel with a finely made thickened rim. Its base is precisely cut, but is small enough that this jar cannot stand on its own bottom. Perhaps there was either some kind of stand made for it, it was set into the ground or it may never have been intended to stand upright.

There is a rectangular gouge just below the widest part of the pot (probably created when the tempering material burned out during firing), a small indentation at the edge of the base and small abrasions on the surface.

Calinescu identified a few partial finger and handprints faintly impressed into the red hematite wash layer, discernible among the other striations. Most of these imprints are concentrated in an area located approximately 10 cm. above the 1 cm. loss in the edge of the base. Hand-shaping marks (ridges in the clay) are visible on the interior as well.

Date

This is a classic late Nagada II form of Polished Red pot (Patch, personal communication), similar to the shapes in the P40 series. Trippel suggested P40a, but P40h, k and p are very similar. P40p is shorter than our example but has exactly the same proportions. We have chosen P40a, which is a bigger pot in all dimensions, but has the exact proportions.

Kaiser writes that this is a new kind of barrel shape that appears in IIc. (1957, p. 72) (He specifically mentions P40c, e, k but our pot is similar). He also mentions the lesser quality of finish of the P40 group that seems to characterize the beginning of IIc to the end of IId and early level III, which matches the surface of this pot exactly. This trait may indicate the trend for there to be fewer workshops making more standardized goods for expanded trade, which required consistent units of measure. The precise form but somewhat cavalier surface treatment of this pot is related to the four Early Dynastic pots in our collection. (See 03.026.2000-03.029.2000). Payne dated P40a to IIb and to IId1. (1992, pp. 187-188) and Patch dates them IIc-IId2. (1991, pp. 497, 483, pl. 21, No. 8 for P40h or k) Wilkinson, 1996, who calls this a barrel-shaped jar (p.105) identifies an example in Matmar grave 5118 (p. 113) at the end of his seriation sequence 2a, which equates to Nagada IIb (-IIc) (pp. 48-49). Hendrickx says that the P ware of IIc, IId1 is characterized by a strong increase of regularly curved jars with a small base. (2005, pp.14-15)

Coll: Lowy

Bibl:
Petrie, 1901
Petrie, 1921
Kaiser, 1957
Lowy catalog, pp. 16-17, No. 12
Patch, 1991
Payne, 1992
Wilkinson, 1996
Mona Trippel, Seminar Report, CSUSB, 2004
Hendrickx, 2005

30. Polished Red Flask
Museum No. 01.002.2003

Height: 8 1/4" (20.5 cm.)
Rim: 2 3/8" (6 cm.)
Neck: 1 7/16" (3.7 cm.)
Base: 1 3/8" (4.6 cm.)

Nile Silt

Nagada Ic-IIa c.3800 BCE

This is an excellent example of a serving piece. One can imagine a liquid being poured from it into a cup during a meal. It has a beautiful shape, is elegantly proportioned (base to height 1:4.5, neck to rim c. 1:1.5) and polished, and is finely made with a sharp-edged flat base, thin walls and a simple everted rim to facilitate pouring. Playing against this formal perfection is diagonal movement on the vessel's surface created by slightly angular burnishing that moves from upper left to lower right. Horizontal marks are visible on the interior of the rim indicating how the top was made. The potting and surface treatment is some of the finest work of Predynastic potters.

The black top appears to have been painted later, since its application is regular, approximately 1 1/2 inches from the rim on both the exterior and interior, not at all characteristic of the irregular black shapes on this type of pottery. It is also matte in appearance and may even cover a repair to the top of the vessel. One can see an irregular line around the top as if the clay there were more absorbent or painted first before the rest of the black was applied. There are signs of irregular firing in the dark mark on the lower part of the pot and a vertical matte area of dull red on a section of the upper two thirds of the surface.

Three chips on the rim reveal the Nile silt fabric.

Date

Similar to P65 and P66 in the Corpus, Patch dates P65c to Ic-IIa and P66 to Ic (personal communication) and in 1991 dated P66a to Ia-Ic. (pp. 482, 491, pl. 11) Hendrickx argues that Ic and IIa are so similar that they do not mark a clear distinction between periods.(1996, p. 39) Payne dates P65a to Ic-IIa. (1992, p. 186) Wilkinson (1996) calls this type a tall vase with a flaring mouth (p. 105) and places the examples he found earlier than the above authors. P65 in Mahasna graves 029 and 045 (p. 115), are placed respectively very early in his seriation category 1a (equating to Nagada Ia) and half way through 1a (equivalent to Nagada Ib) (pp. 51-52). At Mahasna grave 088 (p. 115) P66 is very early in the seriation sequence, equating to Nagada Ia. (pp. 51-52)

Coll: Harer

Bibl:
Petrie, 1921
Patch, 1991
Payne, 1992
Scott, 1992, No. 2B, p.14
Wilkinson, 1996
Hendrickx, 1996

31. Polished Red Flask
Museum No. 01.008.2003

Height: 6 1/2" (16.1 cm.)
Rim: 2" (5 cm.)
Neck (narrowest point): 1 3/8" (3.3 cm.) [1" (2.4cm.) from rim]
Greatest width: 3 3/4" (9.4 cm.)
Base: 7/8" (2.1 cm.)

Nile Silt

Nagada Ic-IIc c.3800-3300 BCE

One of the most beautiful pots in the collection, it is perfectly formed, with base to height proportions of ca. 1:7.5, base to width of ca. 1:4, base to rim of ca. 1:2 and rim to width of ca. 1:2. Its balance and symmetry tell us how skillful the best Predynastic potters were. Petrie illustrates a jar with similar proportions on his chart of the most common types in Diospolis Parva, 1901. Beautifully polished with a regular pattern of vertical burnishing marks about one-eighth inch apart, it has a slightly bulbous body which is countered by its curving tall neck. Because it fits so perfectly in the hand, has a closed mouth, narrow throat, everted neck and delicate rim, it is a perfect vessel from which to pour liquid, perhaps an oil. It probably was a valued piece of dinnerware, but it might have served religious/magical functions, or it may have been intended from the beginning as a grave good.

It has a flat base and there are clear horizontal marks around the opening of the interior, probably made with a piece of leather.

An overall varnish or other consolidant/coating application is indicated by visible brush lines, oriented vertically to blend with original vertical burnish marks. (Calinescu)

Date

There is nothing in the Corpus exactly like this vessel, but there are many with a similar shape and P47a is one of the closest, except it is over two inches shorter than our example. Kaiser says this flask form first appeared in IIb and had previously been made in B ware. (1957, p. 71) On p. 73 he says that the last P flask occurs at Abydos in Ic. Endesfelder dates a similar flask from Armant (grave 1418) to IIb, (1990, p. 111) while Patch dates P47a from IIb to IId2. (1991, pp. 483, 496, pl. 20) Payne suggests IIc, so this is primarily a Nagada II vessel. (1992, p. 187). Wilkinson (1996) agrees. Calling this type a bottle-shaped vase with flaring mouth, he found an example at Matmar grave 5118 (p. 113) located at the end of 2a in his seriation sequence, which equates to Nagada IIc (pp. 48-49).

Coll: Harer

Bibl:
Petrie, 1901
Petrie, 1921
Kaiser, 1957
Endesfelder, 1990
Patch, 1991
Payne, 1992
Scott, 1992, No. 4A, pp. 18-19.
Wilkinson, 1996

32. *Fish Pot
Museum No. EI 01.108.1998

Height: 6 3/4" (17.1 cm.)
Width: 5" (12.7 cm.)
Length: 10 1/2" (26.7 cm.)

Nile Silt (Chaff ware)

Nagada IIc-IId2 c.3650-3300 BCE

This red clay fish has a thickened, slightly everted rim raised above and opening at the top of the body, and lug handles indicating its function as a vessel. The parts of the fish are clearly formed, from its turned-down mouth, eyes and gills (represented by the ridges under the eyes), vertical ridge running down the center of its face, and back fin (probably represented by a slight protrusion between the bottom of the pot and the tail). A top fin is indicated by the raised area between the opening at the top and the tail. Its general shape and appearance is like the tilapia. (See Gamer-Wallert, pl. V)

The tilapia was a very important symbol in the Predynastic. As members of a riverine culture, the ancient Egyptians were familiar with and dependent on fish, a primary source of nutrition throughout Egyptian history. After the annual Nile flood, fish would be left in the evaporating pools as the water receded and were easily available for the taking. More standard fishing techniques developed early, especially netting. Fishhooks in ivory and later in metal are among some of the earliest finds.

When a food source such as fish is so central to one's existence and so plentiful, it has natural associations as something good, pleasant, nourishing – a sign of abundance, prosperity and contentment. From there it can take on spiritual qualities. It literally is a "life sustainer" and we know that later there were fish taboos in some communities, proving the spiritual role fish played in their beliefs – either as a positive or negative force. (Brewer and Friedman, pp. 2, 4, 9) One species of tilapia turns red when it is pregnant and the fertility and birth associations of the color red would reinforce that of the fish shape itself. (Brewer and Friedman, p. 2) Later, red was the color of the sun and the tilapia became one of the guardians who accompanied the solar boat on its journey through the night. (Brewer and Friedman, p. 2) Fish were also associated with chaos of the primordial world, and thus something that had to be conquered to maintain the divine order of things (that is why we see so many fishing scenes in Dynastic art.) (Brewer and Friedman, p. 1)

The Egyptian artisan knew fish well enough to depict actual species. The tilapia is a shallow water fish, easily observed and caught, and still a major food source in Egypt today. They may have chosen this fish because they knew it well and liked it, thus leading to its function as an amulet made from many different materials.

But it may have had a more symbolic meaning. Some species of tilapia protect their eggs by keeping them in their mouths till they hatch. The ancient Egyptian would have seen this birth as a potent fertility symbol, or at least as a sign of "rebirth," so central to Egyptian burial practices and later religious beliefs. Later this mouth-breeding fish was associated with the creator god Atum, who took his seed into his mouth and spit out the world. (Brewer and Friedman, 2)

It is an example of the rare zoomorphic pots made in Predynastic Egypt. Kaiser (1957) excludes these types in his chronological schema so this pot, despite its interest, has not been studied deeply in the literature. There is a similarly shaped pot in Cambridge (Bourriau 1981, No. 41, pp. 31-32), but it is made of a different material and has painted decoration. The Ashmolean example is closer but its mouth is open. (Crowfoot-Payne, 1993, p. 22, Fig. 16, No. 69)

This vessel probably served a special function rather than the daily uses of cooking, serving and eating. It clearly held something important, and its shape directly related to the significance of its contents. It has lug handles, so it could be hung by a string carrier and transported, but such handles are usually found on much smaller jars that were intended to hold precious materials – unguents or perfumes which probably had more of a spiritual/magic function than a cosmetic one. Although larger, this vessel could have functioned in the same way. Also, it may have hung in a special magical or spiritual place or been used during a ritual. Wilkinson (2003, p. 93) stresses the importance of portability of all personal possessions in early Nagada, indicated by the objects with lug handles and punched holes, and these people seem to have moved between the Nile Valley and the surrounding areas on a seasonal basis.

The pot contains interesting information about the nature of sculpture in the Predynastic period. Even in its abraded state, the pot shows the Egyptian artisan adept at naturalistic depiction. The fish is realistic and recognizable, as we would expect from a culture that knew fish so well and depended on them as a food staple.

This pot reveals the techniques used to make it. Inside are clear signs of hand-building, rim turning, slab construction, especially where two slabs meet to form the tail. Also informative are the interior buildup of clay at the spot where the lugs are attached – where the potter's hand held the wall of the pot on the inside to allow the lug to be pressed into the body of the fish. Despite the fact that most of the surface is worn off, there are remnants of slip around the shoulder, on the lips and eyes. The chaff-ware fabric is very clear. Friedman explains that the addition of chaff insures that the clay will be easier to handle in the creation of such

a complicated shape, and that it will not shrink too much as it dries, perhaps even firing more rapidly. (1994, p.267) On one side of the bottom there are two round dark circles, which may be burn marks from when it was fired or was touching something else in the kiln. Reading the physical signs of the potter's activity brings this Predynastic work into our own time – we see the process taking place as if it were made today rather than over 5,000 years ago

Mieke Bahmer provided the starting point for this entry.

Date

Payne dates F68c to Ic, F68a to IIa, F68 to IIc (1992, pp. 186-187) but limits P68 to Nagada II in her Ashmolean catalog. (Payne, 1993, p. 22)

Petrie classified this type of pot as F(Fancy) ware and our example is similar in form to the 68 series in the Corpus, especially close to F68m with its closed mouth. Our pot has a more clearly indicated, down-turned mouth, and the thickened, slightly everted rim opening at the top of the body is raised higher off the body and our lug handles also seem to be placed higher. However ours is red, not buff, like the Corpus example. The suggested tail of the example is just like ours. The Corpus example also shows details that may represent gills or mouth as does our pot.

F (Fancy) ware is a problematic category that has been rejected by most specialists because it is not connected to a specific fabric – only to a judgment about the nature of the shape of the pot.

Coll: Harer

Bibl:

Petrie, 1921
Gamer-Wallert, 1970
Bourriau, 1981
Brewer and Friedman, 1989
Payne, 1992
Payne, 1993
Wilkinson, 2003
Mieke Bahmer, Seminar Report, CSUSB, 2004

33. Wavy-handled Pot
Museum No. 01.009.2003

Height: 10 3/4" (27.2 cm.)
Rim (exterior): 4 3/8" (10.9 cm.)
Rim (interior): 3 1/2" (8.9 cm.)
Rim width: 7/16" (1.1 cm.)
Rim thickness: 5/16" (.8 cm.)
Greatest width (at handles): 3 1/4" (8.4 cm.)
Base: 2 3/8" (6.2 cm.)
Distance of handle from rim: 2" (5.1 cm.)

Marl

Nagada IIIa2 c.3300-3100 BCE

Inscribed in ink: W4EPD on rim

An important type of pot in the history of Predynastic Egyptian ceramics, this piece belongs to a category that Petrie used as the lynchpin of his seriation process and it appears on his chart of most common types. (Petrie, 1901) He discovered a large number of a type of hard-fired, buff vessel that he believed changed shape over time. The earliest ones were big and bulbous with large ledge handles on either side. They have since been found to be Palestinian/Syrian oil jars although the Egyptians copied them too. Petrie believed that over time these vessels "degraded" into ever narrower, cylindrical, more open-mouthed vessels, with the ledge handles getting smaller until they became vestigial, simply designs impressed in the clay. He made this assumption based on observations of vessels found in Early Dynastic graves. Most scholars have accepted his chronology for this ware. It was the mutual exclusiveness of this W ware with the C (Cross-Lined) ware that led Petrie to believe that there was a chronological development of Predynastic pottery and that lay at the basis of his classification system and sequence dates.

Made of marl clay, they probably required a kiln as opposed to the covered fires that most believe were used to fire the pots made of Nile Silt. Marl clay has to be fired at a higher temperature, and it produces harder pots that can better serve as containers for trade goods. Thus a vessel of this material has a slightly higher value than those of Nile Silt.

Apparently this entire class of ware was used to store and transport, as indicated on our pot by the crisscrossed painted lines that stand for what would in earlier times have been a woven net or sling used to carry the pot. The marks on our pot are quickly applied and not perfectly regular. They include a circle that runs around the pot under the rim. Since there are other pots with more complex depictions of this "netting," the lines on our pot seem to be decorative rather than realistic.

The pot's sides are slightly curved, and its rim is quite broad, everted and turned, visually providing a strong cap for the design. It seems too finely made to be used for transportation, and its ledge would easily be chipped or broken, so this pot was probably made to be put into the grave.

Archaeologists report that these pots have a distinct smell when they are found in tombs – some identify a coconut odor – and seem to have held some kind of vegetable or animal fat. (Payne 1993, p. 102) Midway through the development of these pots, the contents were a mixture of fat and mud and by the time our pot appears; they are found at sites filled exclusively with mud. In burials, this practice may have been a practical way to save valuable food resources, or the mud may have had its own significance as well (i.e. representing the land, fertility) or may have symbolically or magically represented the valuable foodstuffs that had been stored in the pots in the earlier period.

Our pot is small for a storage jar and close to W60 in size in the Predynastic Corpus, and slightly smaller than the similarly decorated W63. It is closest to 46H4 in Petrie's Protodynastic Corpus, (pl. VIII) in terms of how the painted decoration is applied to the pot, but the ledge type is placed higher on the Corpus example. Judy Solis identified the vestigial handle as type R from Petrie's Corpus but in his Protodynastic Corpus, 1953, it is identified as type 46b, SD 77, 78, pl. IX . It is coil built with the joins of the coils on the interior right below the wavy handle. The rim of our vessel is cracked and has a 2 1/2" piece of rim broken off and repaired, but it is very symmetrical. The vessel's slightly curving walls and wide lip allow easy filling and emptying of probably liquid contents. About one fourth of the way from the top, appear the characteristic "handle" design made by pushing a finger or some instrument upward on the wet clay body, creating a series of ridges. On our pot there are eleven of these decorative scallop marks. The base, with faint irregular painted lines, is cut flat and has two round sections where an upper layer seems worn away.

There is some abrasion on the surface and buff marks, which are concretion – very common on marl pots. The ink inscription on the rim of the pot may have been made by the archaeologist who excavated it or by the collection or museum that housed it.

Judy Solis provided the starting point for this entry.

Date

All cylindrical W ware is late (Petrie, SD.75-79) or Nagada III and Kaiser (1957) places it only in Nagada IIIa2, the next to the last level of his classification, a period that verges into the Protodynastic. All subsequent specialists place it somewhere in III. (Needler, 1984, p. 216, III; Patch, 1991 dates W62 to IIIa1-IIIb and W60 in IIIa2-IIIb; Payne, 1992, (III) p. 188; Wilkinson (1996) showed several similar pot-types in his seriation group PO50 (p.106). This pot shape without any decoration is common in the Early Dynastic cemetery at Tarkhan: the type that Wilkinson labels as 46 appears in forty-five graves, some with multiple examples (pp.110-112). At Matmar it is found in eleven graves (pp. 112-113), at Mostagedda three times (p 114). The W60 series is found at Mostagedda grave 1660 (p. 114), early in his seriation sequence 2 (p. 50), which is the equivalent of Nagada IIb (p. 49) and at Mahasna, in grave 122 (p. 115), near the end of his sequence 3a (p. 52), which is the same as Nagada IIa2. The pot-type W62 appears in fourteen graves in Hierakonpolis (p. 117), all in his seriation sequence 3 (p. 57) which is equal to Nagada IIIa2-IIIb (p. 56). Hendrickx, 1996, p. 62 and 1999, p. 31 dates W60-62 to IIIa2. In 2005, he identified this type, with its maximum diameter located at the rim, relatively broad base and continuous decorated band as the most characteristic W-ware vessel of IIIa2. (p. 17)

Coll: Harer

Bibl:

Petrie, 1921
Petrie, 1953
Kaiser, 1957
Needler, 1984 For a record of one of the earliest finds of this type of pot, see Henry de Morgan's field notes in Needler, p. 70) Also Figs 15, 17, 20.
Patch, 1991
Payne, 1992
Scott, 1992, No. 4B, pp. 18- 19
Payne, 1993
Wilkinson, 1996
Hendrickx, 1996
Hendrickx, 1999
Judy Solis, Seminar Report, CSUSB, 2004
Hendrickx, 2005

D (DECORATED WARE)

Geometric designs dominate decorated Predynastic pottery, whether scratched into black ware and sometimes filled in with white (Petrie's N-Incised) or painted with a white or yellowish pigment on red (C-Cross-Lined). Most experts believe that such motifs derive from basketry. Floral decoration is common on C ware too and there are some rare figurative pieces with both humans and animals as well. The most uniform figurative pots are those developed in Nagada II, in which red ochre (iron oxide) paint was applied to buff colored clay. Petrie called this D – Decorated ware – and its designs are the most consistent of all Predynastic pottery. It has the same shape, motifs, decoration, and manufacture no matter where in Egypt it is found, but there are varied combinations of its relatively limited repertory of images. This likeness implies a common culture and a sociopolitical uniformity that most specialists see as the first step toward the development of the Egyptian state under a single ruler. (Kemp, 1989, p. 44) Implied is an industrial process, where a handful of workshops produced this ware, and a developed trading and transportation system moved these pieces up and down the Nile. (Smith, 1993, Aksamit, 1996, p. 21) Such pieces are scarce and almost always found in graves, so they were not intended for everyday use. (Friedman, 1994, p. 738) Many specialists see the decoration on D ware as a preliminary step toward the development of writing. (Arnett, 1982, B. Adams in Hoffman, First Egyptians, 1988, p. 53, Finkenstaedt, 1985, citing Fairservis, pp. 85-86, Graff, 2002)

One category of this ware is decorated with regular semi-circular, comma, dot, dash, cross-hatched, checkerboard or spiral designs. Petrie, and most subsequent writers, believe that these were meant to imitate stone vessels, which were more valuable and which eventually, in Dynastic times, replaced pottery as luxury funerary goods. There are some cases where Petrie may be correct – the wavy lines do look like abstractions of the horizontal lines of calcite vases. But Predynastic painters were skilled enough to do a better job of imitation. More likely the designs are early examples of what in Archaic and Dynastic times became important signifiers on their art – names, titles, labels of contents. (Van den Brink, 1992, suggests this as one possible meaning, and his fourth footnote lists all who have suggested this idea, among other interpretations.)

Aksamit (1992, p. 21) and Friedman (1994, p. 203), citing S. P. Harvey's 1987 Yale senior thesis, suggest that there were distinct styles of Decorated ware associated with different workshops. Harvey argues for a local school around Hememieh that produced marl jars of slightly different proportions and decoration from those in the Nagada region. This middle Egyptian painting style was characterized by an asymmetrical treatment of space resulting in vases decorated differently on opposite sides, whereas in Upper Egypt the vases had strict, symmetrical placement on opposites sides of similar motifs. (cited in Friedman, p. 347)

These pots range from small and simple, bearing one or only a few of the standard motifs, like the two squat pots with simple linear decoration (Museum Nos. 03.022.2000 and 03.023.2000). There can be various combinations of a few decorative elements, such as our flamingo pot (Museum No. EL01.062.1998). The most elaborate of these decorated vessels are those that are usually seen depicting boats (Museum No. EL01.042.1998 and EL02.005.2004).

Non-figurative decorated marl pots first appear in early Nagada II, around 3800 BCE, with the most elaborate scenes dating to late Nagada, IIc and d, c.3650-3300 BCE. (Kaiser, 1957, p. 75) This ware category is rare, and from one-third to one-half of it has painted designs (Patch, personal communication). Those with elaborate painted decoration are even rarer. Aksamit says she knows about 200 of the scenes with boats. (1996, p. 17) During this period the variety characteristic of earlier ceramic coarse ware and stone tools was replaced by a common rough ware throughout all of Egypt. (Friedman, 1994, Holmes, 1989). Additionally, graves became richer (Kaiser, 1957, p. 75) – indicating a major socio/economic development in the second half of Nagada II.

Decorated ware seems to have served an elite group for a special purpose. It probably was made for religious/funerary ceremonies and rituals, which must have involved priests or elites who handled these vessels. These same people could have served both political and religious functions as they did in later Dynastic times when members of the elite would devote part of their time to religious service. B. Adams (in Hoffman, 1988, p. 55), says, "It is probable that they were meant to confer special benefits on the dead. Perhaps the often-repeated motifs were simply meant to ensure a continuation of spiritual life in an abundant Nilotic environment; or in a more sophisticated way, they may be spells recording life, death and guaranteed resurrection." When scenes with animals, birds and fish appear, they may suggest hunting as a metaphor. Animals and plants represent nature as an omnipresent, often dangerous force that can be controlled symbolically by isolating them on the surface of the pot – i.e. subjugated on the pot and taken into the grave and the afterlife. Those passing into the afterlife want to be surrounded by familiar nature, yet they also want to be safe. If the various motifs represent aspects of the world, then this imagery may be the first indications of taking all aspects of the known world into the afterlife. Recently, Hendrickx (2000) and Graff (2003) argued that some specific animal images on the vases and their association with other images (the ostrich/flamingo and boat in the former, the addax antelope and the woman in the latter) indicate pot owners' high status.

While there is much discussion about the meaning and significance of the scenes on the decorated pots, everyone recognizes the limited repertory of objects that are combined to form them, although there are multiple suggestions as to what many of these objects represent. (See the list in B. Adams in Hoffman, 1988, pp. 53, 55) The most common suggestions are boats/buildings, cabins/flooring, oars/palisades, a geometric form identified as an animal skin mounted on a post (Hendrickx, 1998, pp. 215-221), and a fan-like shape called a sycamore tree. (Adams in Hoffman, 1988, p. 55) There are water signs, plants – one type appears as a

branch or branches on the stern of the "boat," and standards/insignia with two banners below it, usually attached to the "cabin" on the right side of the "boat." (Payne, 1993, p. 99) Figurative images include flamingos or ostriches, large flying birds seen from the front, other flying birds represented by rows of "z," "s" or "n" marks. The presence of river birds was ubiquitous in ancient Egypt, and many of the animals that appear on these pots and other Predynastic objects are riverine. B. Adams has also called these marks numbers, libation water or weight notations. (Hoffman, 1988, p. 55) Various animals, and male and female figures also appear. Abstract designs include repeated triangles, usually interpreted as hills.

Among the largest and most prominent motifs is what Petrie first referred to as a boat. (Petrie, Naqada and Ballas, p. 12) This large boat typically appears on either side of a pot between the lug handles. Boats were popular motifs because boating on the Nile River was such an important aspect of Egyptian experience, the heart of their communication and trade system. In Dynastic times, a central image in their funerary art was the solar boat, including cabins/shrines; this Predynastic image might be its precursor. The boats may depict transport to burial or cult vessels, if the figures in them are deities. A more practical interpretation is that they were real boats delivering persons or materials, probably in connection with a funerary ceremony. In this view, the main objects on the boat are cabins or removable decking on which people could stand.

Bruce Williams explains the significance of the boat as part of what becomes a set series of pharaonic scenes (Tomb 100, Turin papyrus, Qustul incense burner). (1987, pp. 261-263) He argues that pharaonic iconography developed during this time and that we are probably mistaken in even having the concept of "pre-dynastic." He distinguishes sacred barks with high prows to galleys, such as the ones on this pot.

In 1916-17, Naville proposed that they were buildings surrounded by a palisade or built on stilts. (pl. I between pp. 80 and 81) He made a strong argument, including the fact that early images of boats include clearly defined oars, while the images on these pots do not depict what are thought of as oars in the same way, having no broad attachment at the bottom, as well as showing no one rowing. Also, when there is a large steering oar, it is held in an oarsman's hands and it does have the broad lower section. He provided convincing illustrations and his ideas are still worth considering, since they have recently been revived in a series of articles by Monet-Saleh and El-Yahky. They believe that what most have seen as a boat was actually a political/religious headquarters. If the image were a building, in this case perhaps identifying the ceremonial site, the purpose of the decoration and the pot itself remains the same as if it were a boat, that of serving a funerary ritual.

The 40 standards identified on the boats/buildings may have started as signs of family/tribe/clan that was inextricably tied up with a divine power/protector and a geographical area that progressed as the civilization developed into a community, town and eventually a nome, the ancient Egyptian equivalent of a province or state. B. Adams (in Hoffman, p. 55) thinks they are "divine emblems and perhaps also as ensigns of clans or nomes." She mentions that the "X" and the "⟷" are respectively the later Dynastic symbols of the divinities Neith and Min. One problem with the tribal/territorial interpretations is that sometimes different standards appear on the same pot (such as one in our collection), and different ones appear on objects from the same cemetery (i.e. community), which suggests a more personal meaning. They may represent family totems and two on one pot might indicate that two families have joined, either through marriage or adoption. Another possibility is that one symbol represents a specific deity whose origins lie elsewhere. (Patch, personal communication).

Of equal importance to the "boat/building" and usually seen in conjunction with it is a large plant, usually referred to as the "Nagada Plant." Usually the same size as the boat/building, it is often placed at 90 degrees to it on opposite sides of a pot under each lug. Given the importance of agriculture for the Predynastic Egyptians, the significance of plants in terms of fertility, regeneration and sustenance are obvious, and could support the notion of some kind of religious or cultic ceremony involving plant fertility, such as insuring good harvests. Arnett argues for the idea that this form depicts a pot with liquids, possibly libations, pouring into or out of it. Such libations were standard aspects of religious rituals and suggest again the cultic function of these pots. (1982, pp. 7-8, pls. III, IV)

The plant appears to be growing out of a root ball or pot, which can have a variety of forms. A number of curving branches emerge from a central stem and form an overall shape of a truncated circle or oval. The stem then continues upward to form a large curving branch or blossom that has leaves or buds on both sides of it, and then terminates in what may be a flower. The exact nature of the plant is much discussed. It was first identified as an aloe by Schweinfurth (1883, cited in El Hadidi) because modern day Egyptians place pots of aloe on graves or in front of doors – they can live for a long time without water, their sap is healing, so they can represent survival and eternal life. Tackholm (V. Tackholm, The Plant of Naqada, Annales du Service des Antiquités de l'Egypte 51, 1951, 299-312) suggests ***ensete edulis***, (wild banana), a common marshy plant currently grown as an important food source. (Payne, 1993, p. 100) The most recent suggestion by El-Hadidi, 1992, is Halfa Grass (***Desmostachya bipinnata (L.) Stapf***), a common weed in Egypt and a frequent find in Predynastic sites. His illustration of the plant, fig. 3, p. 325 makes a strong case. Also Halfa grass was used extensively in ancient Egypt. (Patch, personal communication)

One of the most puzzling motifs on the pots is a geometric form, usually the third most prominent object in size after the "boat/building" and the Nagada plant. It is symmetrical, with a central axis, usually with an angular finial-like element at the top. Placed on either side of this axis are lines that form a trapezoidal shape, inside of which, at top and bottom are diagonal lines. Since lines inside of shapes are thought to represent basketry, or weaving, this object has been variously interpreted as a sail (made of reed matting), and a trap (like the later Dynastic snap-traps used to catch birds and often seen from above as this one would be). The shape is also similar to an animal skin, with the four pointed corners representing the animal's legs. One of the most recent studies calls it "an animal skin hung on two crossed sticks". (Hendrickx, 1998, pp. 215-221, Graff, 2002, 38)

Occasionally there is a spiral on the bottom of the outside of the vessel like those that appear at the bottom of woven baskets or clay pots, indicating where the maker began working. (Payne, 1993, p. 101) The spiral also forms a major non-figurative motif on D ware. B. Adams says the spiral represents nummulitic limestone, bread, the phrase "surround everything" or is simply decoration. (in Hoffman, 1998, p. 55) The repeated parallel lines, often at oblique angles, that fill in a form are also like the designs in C and N ware, as are the branch and plant forms, triangles and abstracted animals. Even some of the animal and human figures common on D ware first appear in C ware, such as the woman with long hair and arms raised above her head, but they are extremely rare.

Wilkinson (1999, p. 34) argues convincingly that the decoration hints as "the relationship between ... human, natural and supernatural spheres," suggesting a parallel to similar themes in developing notions of divine kingship in Nagada II, thus placing the decoration on the pots securely within the religious and political context of its time.

Graff (2005) recently wrote a semiotic study that argued against reading any of the imagery on Predynastic pots as anecdotes from real life, referring to specific funerary practices. She considers the imagery as a language that needs to be translated. Apparently a major dichotomy exists between the large mammal with twisted horns (identified as an addax, a type of Saharan antelope) and woman on one hand (Graff, 2002), and the Nagada plant and the animal skin hanging on two crossed sticks on the other. She relates these pairings to later pharaonic thought concerning the renewal of life for the dead. Hendrickx (2000) anticipated these ideas in a study of ostrich/flamingo imagery on D-ware that suggested parallels between military/religious symbolism in the Predynastic and pharaonic imagery. Graff argues that there is a parallel between the structures of these paintings and the syntax of the written language of the Old Kingdom. She does not think this Nagada painting is writing, but a "preliminary graphic system" necessary to the development of writing, a proto-syntax rather than a catalog of signs.

34. *Decorated Boat Pot
Museum No. El01.042.1998

Height: 7 1/4" (18 cm.)
Rim: 5 1/2 "(13.8 cm.)
Rim width: 5/8" (1.6 cm.)
Rim thickness: 3/16" (.5 cm.)
Greatest width: 6" (15.2 cm.)
Lug to Lug: 6 3/4" (17.1 cm.)
Base: 2 1/4" (5.5 cm.)
Lug width: 1 1/2" (3.8 cm.); 1 5/16" (3.3 cm.)
Distance from rim to lug: 1" (2.6 cm.)

Nagada IIc c.3650-3500 BCE

Marl

This is a characteristic example of Predynastic decorated Egyptian pottery. All these pots were globular, with lug handles and flat, everted rims. The rim on this pot is flat and one can see clearly where it was attached. On the interior, the rim is one-half inch thick. On the exterior, the bottom of the lid is curved and undercut with a sharp instrument, creating a clear groove, where the rim meets the body. This pot appears on Petrie's chart of most common types in Diospolis Parva, 1901.

The major decoration is on the sides of the pot, but there is also painting on the rim and bottom. Wavy lines run around the rim, which probably indicate water, the geographical context for the imagery on the pot. The decoration on the bottom is a spiral, a common motif on decorated pottery, usually interpreted as replicating the patterns found on stone vessels made out of patterned stone. (Scott, 1986, p. 35, Nos. 13A, 13B) But there are many other possible meanings for the spiral. It is like the spiral shape at the bottom of woven baskets that are believed to have influenced clay pots, where a similar shape is often found on the inside of the base of hand-built pots. It may identify what the pot was to hold, either a liquid, perhaps with a surface that has been stirred, or a substance that started out as a liquid, such as animal or vegetable fat poured into the pot where it solidified. It was a shape associated with ponds or waterholes in the earlier Cross-Lined ware.(Finkenstaedt, 1985, pp. 85-86) In Dynastic times it was a convention for a coil of rope, especially the cordage of a ship. The word that ultimately meant "to enclose or surround" probably deriving from both the idea and depiction of rope. (ibid., p. 86) It might also represent a river eddy.

The largest objects covering the broadest part of the pot between the two lugs on either side are boats. There is always an arching form at one end, interpreted as a plant, such as a palm branch, perhaps providing shade or serving as a sail (Thomas, p. 97), and vertical poles near the structures, upon which is a standard.

This pot was probably made in Nagada because it has the "balanced" composition with boats on either side of the top of the pot, between the lug handles, while under them are the animal skin motif and on either side, under the lugs, are large "Nagada plants." On the left side, the boat has 23 oars, a space that is equal to that existing between the two structures on the boat, then 18 oars on the right. On the other side that has the fan shape (sycamore tree) underneath, there are 20 oars on the left and 18 on the right, while both "cabins" have six horizontal lines. The standard on this side of the boat is a common one, like a squeezed "z," made up of a horizontal line with shorter lines at each end forming acute angles, with two angular lines below it, probably a banner. The opposing boat has a different standard, one that looks like a downward curving, concave branch with a bud on the end. Part way down and crossing the vertical post is an irregular convex line, curved in the opposite direction.

Below the boat is an animal skin, a fairly large and complex form that is very common on these pots. (Petrie, 1921, p. 21, Arnett, 1982, p. 16, pl XIV, Monet-Saleh, 1983, pp. 193-194, Payne, 1993, p. 91, Graff, 2002, p. 38)

On the side of the pot, there are four flying bird motifs above the ledge handles on both sides of the pot and four vertical lines on one ledge handle and four horizontal lines on the other. There is also a water line placed at an angle under one ledge. Below each lug handle is a large "Nagada plant." On either side of the central vertical stalk sprout curving branches, one above the other. On this pot there are 10 branches on the left side and nine on the right of one of these plants, with a vertical water line to the side, and on the opposite side of the pot there are nine branches on each side. This plant seems to grow out of a container shaped like a narrow triangle with its single point facing down, and it has four horizontal lines in it.

Between the lug handle and the rim is a very common form – a horizontal line with a small vertical "bump" in the middle, in this case with a row of short vertical lines under it. These horizontal lines are usually interpreted as birds in flight. (Payne, 1993, p. 101 following Petrie) They represent birds seen straight on, so that one only sees the edges of their wings with the body in between (in this case depicted by the jog made in the horizontal line).

The jar has broad indentations on opposite sides of the pot. These flattened areas are probably the result of pots leaning against each other during the drying process. There is a small hole drilled in the base.

Date

Our pot is the same size as Petrie's Corpus D43a, with a sequence date of 45-63, which covers Nagada II and the beginning of Nagada III. Our imagery is like 41b, j, n and s. Kaiser places these pots in Nagada IIc and IId1, or middle Nagada II and says that the first images of boats occur on D ware in IIc. (1957, p. 75) Payne places all these in IIc. (1990, pp. 78, 79; 1992, p. 187); 1993, p. 106, Nos. 852, 854, 856) Wilkinson (1996) locates a similar pot in Mahasna, grave 133 (p. 116) at the end of his seriation sequence 2b (p. 52) which equates to Nagada IId2 (p. 51) Hendrickx writes that in IIc Decorated ware is dominated by relatively small flat-based regularly curved jars with lug handles, with characteristic figurative decoration. By IId2 such pots hardly ever occur and figurative representation is almost completely missing. (2005, pp. 14, 16)

Coll: Harer

Bibl:

Petrie, 1921
E.S. Thomas "The Branch on Prehistoric Ships," Ancient Egypt, IV, 1923, p. 97
Kaiser, 1957
Arnett, 1982
Monet-Saleh, 1983
Adams in Hoffman, 1988
Payne, 1990
Payne, 1992
Payne 1993
Friedman, 1994
Wilkinson, 1996
Hendrickx, 2005

35. *Decorated Boat Pot
Museum No. El 02.005.2004

Height: 6 1/2" (15.6 cm.)
Rim Exterior: 2 7/8" (7.1 cm.)
Rim Interior: 2" (4.9 cm.)
Rim Thickness: 3/16" (.4 cm.)
Greatest width :3 3/4" (9.4 cm.)
Base:13/16" (2.2 cm.)
Lugs: 3/4" (1.8 cm.) wide at greatest height, 15/16" (2.2 cm.)where attached to pot

Nagada IIc-IId c.3650-3300 BCE

Marl

This slender pot is covered with clear images from the standard repertory of decoration for this ware. The paint is applied darker in some areas, lighter in others and forms a well-balanced and ordered decoration, with similar images on both sides. Such an arrangement indicates that this vessel was probably made in Nagada. (Harvey cited in Friedman, 1994, p. 347)

On one side there is as large boat placed between the two lugs. Two cabins rest on it and there is a "supine Z" standard attached to the cabin on the right, similar to one on the pot discussed above. The left cabin is made up of five horizontal lines, the right one with four. There are two branches at the back of the boat, the left one marked with 14 lines, the one to the right of it with ten. There are 17 "oars" on the left side of the boat, 14 on the right.

Below the boat is a large, clear animal skin motif with three wavy "water" lines below it that encircle the entire pot at the bottom and seem to continue on the base. The skin has five angular lines at the top of its left side and five below, while on the right there are six angular lines at the top and four at the bottom.

On the verso the scene repeats itself with the same standard, two cabins, but with three branches at the back of the boat, the one farthest to the left marked with 11 lines, the branch next to it with eight, and the one at the right with seven. The animal skin has five lines at the top and four at the bottom, while on the right it has six at the top and four at the bottom.

On each side of the pot, under the lugs is a large Nagada plant. It sits in what looks like a square container, or perhaps a cabin, since it looks like those objects on the boats. On one side there are eight branches to the plant and 10 on the right, with the large stem curving over to the right, with 18 leaves on top and 12 on the bottom, and the plant ends in a double "c." At the lower left and right corners of the plant are cabin signs, the one on the left with the top of its vertical sides leaning to the right, and on the right; these vertical parts curve to the left, "framing" the plant like parentheses.

On the other side there is a similar pot and the plant has nine lines on the left and 11 on the right and "framing" cabins are placed at the lower left and right as already described on the other side.

The two barrel lugs, which are attached one inch from the rim, are decorated as well, each with three wavy horizontal lines, and there are another three wavy horizontal lines between the rim and the lug. There is one wavy line running around the rim.

On the lower part of the pot, under one of the Nagada plants, are ridges as if someone had shaved off clay with vertical strokes in order to narrow the shape. Inside there is a kind of ledge around the circumference where the top was turned, at the same place where the wavy lines are placed on the outside of the pot. Also on the inside is a horizontal mark where the rim is attached, and a horizontal gouge was made on the inner circumference at the level where the lugs attach..

This pot clearly establishes the "watery" environment for the boat and the Nagada plant. The large animal skins and Nagada plants accompany the boats as if following a pattern. In fact the entire pot seems formulaic, very orderly and balanced. This regularity is what leads one to think of this imagery as a kind of language carrying a specific message.

There is a crack running from one of the lugs to the rim.

Date

The same height as Petrie 47g but not as wide, with decoration like 41b (SD 46) and 41s. Patch dates it to IIc (Patch, personal communication) Payne, 1992 dates D41 to IIc-IId1, pp. 187-188. Hendrickx places these decorated pots primarily in IIc but notes rare appearance in IId2. (2005, pp.14,16)

Coll: Harer

Bibl:
(See EL 01.042.1998)

36. *Flamingo Pot
Museum No. EI 01.062.1998

Height: 5" (12.7 cm.)
Rim: 5" (12.7 cm.)
Greatest width: 4 15/16" (12.3 cm.)
Base: 1 7/16" (3.6 cm.)
Lug width: 2 3/4" (6.8 cm.)
Distance of lug from rim: 1/2" (1.2 cm.)
Rim width: 3/8" (1 cm.)

Nagada IIc-IId1 c.3650-3300 BCE

Marl

This small, decorated pot is cylindrical with a flat bottom and a gentle curve connecting the bottom to the sides. It has two lug handles at the top, which indicates that it was designed to be hung and on some kind of cord. It curves in above the lugs to an everted rim with a flat top.

Decoration covers the entire jar. There are two wavy lines on the rim, connected at one point with a perpendicular line, three on one lug handle and three or four on the other. The scene of flamingos is framed by them as well. On the base are three wavy lines in a circle. A similar design appears on the bottom of a pot decorated with flamingo imagery in the Ashmolean Museum (Payne, 1993, Fig. 45, No. 879) and on a number of decorated pots in the Yale University Art Gallery. (Scott, 1986, p. 31, No. 9; p. 34, No. 12; p. 35, No. 13C) Most specialists think these represent water (and in later, Dynastic times, the hieroglyph for water was a short wavy line), and such a meaning is appropriate for these marsh dwellers. There are six lines above the flamingos covering the top 1 1/4-inches of the pot, and five on the bottom, whose edge is much worn, covering 1 1/4 inches of the vessel. In contrast to the more elaborate boat pots, the images line up in a row, as if to foreshadow the registers that characterize Dynastic visual imagery. Of course, flamingos travel in flocks, and the decoration may be depicting that fact. The eleven flamingos cover a field 21/4 inches tall, and are made up of simplified, abstract shapes: the head is a curlicue, sometimes thickened at the top as it meets the vertical that forms the neck. Sometimes this line continues down to form the front leg, but usually the legs are placed further back from the neck. About half-way down the vertical, a half circle forms the body and a second vertical begins below this form and parallels the first "leg." The two legs are always parallel and close to one another. Sometimes the "bodies" overlap slightly. These two shapes and two lines combine to form a surprisingly naturalistic depiction of an object from the real world that they knew so well. Evidently these images were so highly conventionalized that sometimes the bodies did not have the proper number of legs. (Hendrickx, 2000, p. 32) On our pot the eleven flamingos have the correct number.

What all these pots have in common is that they are small, and they may have had a ritual purpose, probably involving some kind of liquid they held. The flamingo's significance (symbiosis with the marshy river banks, fishing skill, survival and reproduction, association with the Nile Valley) was transferred to the contents of the jar. There are jars on which there is only one flamingo, and then there are flamingos in rows, in which there are never less than three of the birds.

Hendrickx (2000) recently proposed that these animals may be ostriches or a purposeful combination of attributes of both this bird and the flamingo that functions on a symbolic or semiotic level (p.31), although he focuses his discussion on decorated pots that associate the birds with boats. (pp. 43, 45-57)

The rim is scraped and chipped, which may be signs of use. There is a crack 1 1/4 inches from the rim down the body and some irregularities of color and surface in the marl clay, perhaps from wear and age. On the inside, there are clear horizontal marks as if the surface were scraped with a tool.

Date

This small decorated pot is not exactly the size of anything in the Corpus, nor is it like anything in Payne's Chronology (1990), but it has a shape like Corpus D89, which is 41/2 inches tall. Its decoration, a row of flamingos, is like D53g in the Corpus, a pot close in size at 4 7/8 inches tall. The two pots with rows of flamingos that Payne does picture (D50 and D55) are both IId1 (1993), the same date suggested by Payne, 1992, p. 188.

Coll.: Harer

Bibl:
Petrie, 1921
Payne, 1990
Payne, 1992
Payne, 1993
Hendrickx, 2000

SQUAT JARS

There are four similar jars in our collection, in varied sizes and states of preservation, but sharing shape and decoration. These small elongated or globular pots fit nicely in the hand. All have lug handles but it is not clear that they were meant to be suspended. They probably had special meaning and were made for a religious, ritualistic, magical, medical purpose or all the above. Originally they were covered with wavy horizontal lines running from top to bottom, and such lines may depict the weave of basketry, but are usually interpreted as water signs. Such regular linear rows may have indicated the jars' contents, since such labels were common on Archaic and Dynastic pots. A similar function for pot marks has been suggested as well. (Van den Brink, 1992, p. 276, fn 4.) The shape and rim have already suggested liquids or something that solidified from a liquid state, such as oil or fat. The regular arrangement of vertical marks on the rim could indicate the contents of the jar pouring over the rim.

Some of these pots have decorated rims that contrast strongly with the rest of the pot. The rims have clear patterns on them made up of concentric circles at each edge of the rim with thick vertical marks placed regularly between them. The paint is so much clearer than that on the body of the jar that we believe them to be modern. We know that undecorated buff ware that is authentically Predynastic was often painted in modern times. (Payne, 1977, 1993)

Marl

Nagada IIb-IId2 c.3700-3300 BCE

Coll: Lowy

Bibl:
Petrie, 1921
Payne, 1990

37. Squat Jar
Museum No. 03.022.2000

Height: 5 1/8" (13 cm.)
Rim: 2 11/16" (6.8 cm.)
Lug to Lug: 3/8" (8.6 cm.)
Rim width: 3/8" (1 cm.)
Lugs start 7/8" (2.2 cm.) below rim
Lug width: 3⁄4" (1.9 cm.)
Base: 15/16" (2.4 cm.)

Nagada IIc-IId1 c.3650-3300 BCE

The largest of this group of small pots, it is in the poorest condition. It is not well-made: not quite symmetrical, bulging more on one side than the other, with the lugs placed unevenly. Its proportions are width to height, 1:75, base to width, 1:3.5 and base to rim 1:3. This jar may have a violent history since it is in such poor shape. It may have been in a fire because its lower half is covered with burn marks that occurred after the pot was decorated, so the wavy lines probably went all around the pot. It has heavy abrasions on the top three-quarters of the vessel and is mashed in two places, probably before it was fired. There is damage on one side just below and to the right of one of the lugs, and the other is below the rim, just above and to the left of the other lug. Inside, it may have lost its original surface – the current one is rough and the entire surface is covered with concretion, the beige colored calcium and limestone residue that results from burial. Currently it cannot stand on its flat base.

This jar has 21 wavy horizontal lines running from top to bottom, and the specific number of lines could have meant something, but were probably decorative, simply filling the available space. This pot is an example of the strong contrast between the decoration on the body and the rim mentioned above: The faint design on the body and the clear, strong pattern on the rim, made up of concentric circles at each edge with thick vertical marks placed regularly between them.

Date

It is close to D8m in the Corpus, with a sequence date of 46, 47, which is middle Nagada II. Payne places this type of D ware in IIb. (1990, pp 78-79) Wilkinson (1996) found similar pots in Matmar, Mostagedda and Hierakonpolis. The Matmar example was in grave 3077 (p. 113) in the middle of his seriation sequence 1 (p. 50) which equates to Nagada Ic (p. 49). At Mostagedda grave 1643 (p. 114) it is early in his sequence 2 (p. 50) which is equivalent to Nagada IIb (p. 49) and at Hierakonpolis (p. 118) it is at the end of sequence 1 (p. 58), which is the same as Nagada IId1.

Bibl:
Lowy catalog, p. 21, No. 22
Wilkinson, 1996

38. Squat Jar
Museum No. 03.023.2000

Height: 3 3/8 – 4 1/8" (8.5 – 11.4 cm.) irregular
Rim, exterior: 3 3/8" (8.5 cm.)
Rim width: 1/2" (1.3 cm.)
Lug to Lug: 5 1/2" (14 cm.)
Distance of lug from rim: 3/4" (1.9 cm.)

Nagada IIb-IId1 c.3650-3300 BCE

The pot, covered with horizontal wavy lines, has a shape similar to the Polished Red squat jar (03.025.2000). Like 03.022.2000, it also seems to have modern decoration on its rim – a pattern made of clear concentric circles connected by a row of vertical lines, giving the impression of a "plaid" design. Its function and use is similar to those discussed in the previous squat and decorated jars.

It has a gouge repair near the top, concretion on the outside and an irregular surface on the interior.

Date

Like D9c in the Corpus, SD 40-52, it is dated Nagada II. Payne, on the other hand, placed D9c in Nagada IIb. (1990, pp. 78-79; 1992, p. 187; 1993, p. 103, No. 814) Patch dates D9c to IIc and D9g to IIc – IId1. (Patch, personal communication) Wilkinson (1996) identifies this type at Matmar, grave 3067 (p. 113) in the middle of his seriation sequence 2b (p. 48) which equates to Nagada IIc-IId1 (p. 49).

Bibl:
Lowy catalog, pp. 21-22, No. 23
Payne, 1992
Payne, 1993
Wilkinson, 1996

39. Squat Jar
Museum No. 03.024.2000

Height: 2 1/2" (6.3 cm.)
Rim: 2 1/4" (5.7 cm.)
Lug to lug: 3 1/2" (8.9 cm.)

Nagada IIb-IId1 c.3650-3300 BCE

Like 03.023.2000 except smaller, this jar raises similar issues. Its proportions are height to width of 1:1.5 and height to rim, 1:1, so it is a globular, squat, tiny jar. Despite its current condition, it was probably an attractive vessel when new.

Although in poor condition, it seems to have originally had 13 lines from top to bottom. The worn rim has slight traces of two lines. Both lugs had three lines painted on them.

This pot has paint traces on its chipped rim and a big piece off the bottom. There may have been paint on the curved bottom of the pot, but it is so worn that one can't be sure. There is concretion both inside and outside the pot.

Date

Similar in size to Corpus D9g, which Patch dates to IIc-IId1 and in decoration to D9c, dated to IIc. (Patch, personal communication) Petrie places these in Nagada I, II and the beginning of III. Payne, 1990 and 1993 place it in IIb. (See 03.023.2000).

Bibl:
Lowy catalog, p. 22, No. 24
Payne 1993

40. Squat Jar
Museum No. 01.010.2003

Height: 4 1/16" (10.2 cm.)
Rim exterior: 2 1/8" (5.3 cm.)
Rim width: 5/16" (.8 cm.)
Distance from rim to lug: 1/2" (1.1cm.) on one side, 3/4" (1.7cm.) on the other
Greatest width: 3 3/8" (8.5 cm.)
Lug to lug: 3 3/8" (8.5 cm.)
Lug width: 3/4" (1.7 cm.)
Base: 15/16" (2.2 cm.)

Nagada IId1-IId2 c.3300 BCE

This is similar to other pots in our collection, with its bulbous shape, flat rim and lug handles. The rim was cut underneath and forms a sharp transition with the body of the pot. Like our similar pots, it has red-ochre decoration of horizontal lines covering the exterior but the most prominent lines are not the usual wavy ones that we think represent water. Each line is horizontal with a small vertical "jog" in the middle. This type of line is a common motif on decorated pots (See D15 in the Corpus [SD 44]) and Petrie suggested that it represents a bird in flight seen head on. (cited in Payne, 1993, p. 101) The wings are the two horizontal lines and the body is abstracted into the small vertical "jog" that connects them.

Birds were as common as fish in the Nile River valley. They were harder to catch, but Egyptians eventually were able to hunt and trap them for food. In later Dynastic visual imagery, birds were seen as symbols of the destructive forces of nature, and scenes of bird catching or bird hunting were meant to illustrate the tomb owner's role in overcoming forces of disorder. Since almost all Predynastic visual imagery is highly abstracted, the idea that we could be seeing birds and even some idea of dangerous forces in nature on this pot is worth consideration. That decoration like this served a magical/religious function, rather than being dinner ware, explains its rarity.

This pot's decoration is not like anything in the Corpus although it combines elements seen in the D11, D12 and D20 series; that is, sections of similar lines placed on different parts of the pot with space between them. Our pot has two wavy lines on the rim, five horizontal lines on one lug, four on the other.

The top half of the pot has a very regular, symmetrical design: nine lines of the flying bird motif on one side, eight on the other covering the top two inches of the surface. Three wavy watermarks connect them on each side inside the two lugs. This leaves a triangular space in which each lug sits (the triangle is clearer on one side than the other).

The bottom half of the pot has a syncopated design, off-center in comparison to the design on the upper half. There are three angular lines moving from upper left to lower right on half the pot. They connect to six flying bird motifs that cover the lower fourth of the vessel. This leaves a large blank horizontal area about three-quarters of the way around the pot. Opposite it, nine straight lines angle slightly from lower left to upper right, covering nearly half the pot, leaving an upside-down triangular space on the bottom and a left-leaning triangular space where the three angular lines mentioned at the beginning of this paragraph start..

On the base, there are three faint vertical red lines that continue onto the body of the pot for a short distance. Such lines are common on decorated ware. (Scott, 1986, p. 33) There are also some dark marks on the bottom that are probably recent.

The overall effect of the design is a linear patchwork with strong triangular areas of negative space that reaffirm the surface of the pot and create an accent and a counterpoint to the linear patterns. The design is rich and sophisticated and reveals an experimental side of Predynastic design.

The rim seems to have been decorated with two concentric circles, but it is now chipped and much worn, as is the vessel's surface.

Amy Younger provided the starting point for this entry.

Date

With its small size and 1:1 proportions it is close to Dllc or D12b in the Corpus that Patch dates IId1-IId2 (personal communication). Payne, 1992, p. 188 places the former in IId1.

Coll: Harer

Bibl:
Petrie, 1921
Payne, 1992
Scott, 1992, cat. No. 4C, pp. 18-19
Amy Younger, Seminar Report, CSUSB, 2004

LATE WARE JARS

Our four jars are approximately the same size and share a shape that is bulbous, short-necked, with thickened, slightly everted or rolled rims. Their proportions are similar too, with a base to height relationship of 1:3, base to rim of around 1:1.5, base to width either 1:2 or 1:3. They are all quickly made by hand, with the rims attached so rapidly that they are not always centered or even. Often thick turning marks are visible on the interior of the rim. They are all made of marl clay, cleanly potted in terms of their shape, although sometimes irregular with one side more curved than the other, and neatly cut bases. The firing methods achieved the higher temperatures required for firing marl clay, but must not have been carefully controlled because the mix of colors caused by irregular temperatures is common on these pots.

They exemplify the decline in quality in ceramic ware as the period of political unification took place in Nagada III. The centralization of political control meant the industrialization of production, larger workshops were possible that made greater numbers of standardized objects at cheaper prices. Ceramics was no longer the luxury ware that it had been at the beginning of the Predynastic. Now stone vessels were the most highly prized containers, while ceramics became a utilitarian ware.

This group of Late ware pots suggests that the potters of this period knew how to produce standardized sizes and shapes. As the economy became more complex, precise standards of measurement were required with which to set or change prices (especially in a barter system). While pot size became standardized, details of the pot, such as the rim, became less important, as long as it was functional.

All these pots are characteristic of marl vessels buried in tombs, where ochre colored minerals, called concretion, attached themselves to the exterior and interior surfaces.

The early part of Nagada III was a period when Dynastic rulers identified with Dynasty I are known. Hendrickx identifies the time period of IIIa-b as that of Irj and Hor/Ka. (1996, p. 64) Wilkinson (1996) suggests that the rulers of this time are anonymous, and that it is in IIIb that we find the powerful regional rulers such as Scorpion and Ka, identified as "Dynasty O" while the following levels of IIIc-d cover the period from c3100 to beyond 2900 BCE, that is, all of Dynasties I and II. (p. 12) Our pots are from the transition between Predynastic and the following period, variously called Archaic, Early Dynastic, Protodynastic or Dynasty I.

Marl

IId-IIIa2 c.3300-3100 BCE

Coll: Lowy

Bibl:

Petrie, 1921
Petrie, 1953
Kaiser, 1957
Kelly, 1976, pl. 4.12
Payne, 1992
Hendrickx, 1996
Wilkinson, 1996

41. Late Ware Jar
Museum No. 03.026.2000

Height: 7 3/4" (19.6 cm.)
Rim: 4" (10.1 cm.)
Greatest width: 7 1/2" (19 cm.)
Base: 2 3/4" (7 cm.)

This beautifully shaped bulbous vessel has a short neck and thickened, slightly everted rim. Because of its small size and precise shape it may have been used for serving at table, and its rim would have facilitated pouring. It is light olive/beige, with a smooth but unpolished and now badly eroded surface on the top part of the vessel, including the inside and outside of the neck and rim. While it is made of marl clay, it is considered Early Dynastic rough ware. (Patch, personal communication) Patch also identified this vase as a classic Nagada III form.

Around the neck are remnants of some dark marks that may be paint. Many of these pots bear such marks, which were probably indicators of their contents.

Date

It is almost exactly the same size and exact proportions (rim to base, 2:1; base to greatest width 1:3.25) as L59d in the Corpus, which is late Nagada III. Patch thinks it is in the L53 series, which dates IIc-IIIa2 (personal communication). Kaiser places one close to it in Nagada IIIb, the next to the last sequence that is already in a Protodynastic period. (1957, pl. 24) Payne dates some pots from the L53 series in IId1, while L59d is put in III. (1992, p. 188)

Bibl:
Lowy cat., p. 23, No. 26

42. Late Ware Jar
Museum No. 03.027.2000

Height: 5 15/16" (15.1 cm.)
Rim: 2 15/16" (7.4 cm.)
Greatest width: 5" (12.7 cm.)
Base: 2 1/8" (5.4 cm.)

This pot appears balanced and symmetrical, but like so many from this period it is slightly lop-sided on closer inspection. It served its function well, was hard, would not break easily and was readily available, probably at a reasonable price. It is heavily calcified and has dark painted marks on a small section that runs from the neck, one third of the way down the side of the pot. These marks, so common on Protodynastic pots, may indicate its owner or contents. Finger marks remain inside from the process of attaching the thickened rim to the shoulder of the pot.

Date

It is in the L53 series, similar to L53k. Kaiser places it in Nagada IIIb, the last period in his sequence. (1957, pl. 24) It is like 92S (CA6.1) in the Protodynastic Corpus. (1953, pl. XXVIII) Patch dated L53 to IIc-IIIa1 (1991, pp. 508, 552, pl. 50), but now follows Hendrickx with a date range of IId-IIId (Patch, personal communication). Payne puts L53k in IId1. (1992, p. 188) Wilkinson (1996) calls this pot-type a small rounded jar with narrow neck and flat base (p. 108). He finds an example at Mostagedda grave 1752 (p. 114) early in his seriation sequence 3 (p. 50), which is equivalent to Nagada IIIa2 (p. 49). Hendrickx (2005, p. 15) places it in IId2 mentioning that Late ware increases in importance at this time.

Bibl:
Lowy catalog, p. 23, No. 27
Patch, 1991
Hendrickx, 2005

43. Late Ware Jar
Museum No. 03.028.2000

Height: 7 3/4" (19.6 cm.)
Rim: 3 7/8" (9.8 cm.)
Greatest width: 6 1/2" (15.8 cm.)
Base: 2 1/2" (6.4 cm.)

Most of the body of this jar is so well formed and symmetrical (notice the crisp base) that it is surprising to find the upper part and rim so irregular. Earlier in the Predynastic, a pot with a rim as misshapen as this one would not have served as grave goods, and would have eventually been broken up because of heavy use. Such a pronounced, misshapen rim, with clear signs of turning inside the neck, is common in Late ware. The mix of colors, here a light reddish/orange and ochre is characteristic as well. This pot has a clear ridge running around the top where the rim was attached to the body.

There is a scratch on the body and two chips on the lip of the rim.

Date

Like the other Late ware pots in the collection, this is close to L59d in the Corpus, dating within the transition between the Pre- and Protodynastic periods. There is nothing exactly like it in the Protodynastic Corpus. Kaiser (1957, pl. 24) places the type in Nagada IIIb, the last of his sequences. Patch dates this to IId2 (Patch, personal communication) while Payne places it in III. (1992, p. 188)

Bibl:
Lowy catalog, pp. 23-24, No. 28

44. Late Ware Jar
Museum No. 03.029.2000

Height: 6 1/2-6 11/16" (16.4-16.9 cm.)
Rim: 3 3/8" (8.5 cm.)
Greatest width: 5 1/2" (13.9 cm.)
Base: 2 1/8" (5.3 cm.)

Unlike the other pots in this group, this one has no obvious deformation. It is of similar size and proportions to the other three, and probably functioned in the same way. It is distinctive because of the black or dark red splotches (made with finger tips?) irregularly placed on the surface, which could be decorative, or imitative of some material, such as stone. Similar decoration appears on Decorated ware and a Wavy-Handled pot in the Ashmolean Museum. (Payne, 1993, fig. 37, Nos. 827, 832-834 and fig. 50, No. 925) The "dotted" decoration is like D6s or t, whose form parallels Late ware. (Patch, personal communication)

Also of interest is the clear ridge created when the neck was applied to the body. There is also an irregular line where the slip was applied to the body but did not go all the way up the neck of the pot. This vessel also has a perfectly rounded rim with a clear indentation underneath.

Date

Patch dates L59d to IId2-IIIb (1991, pp. 538, 551, pl. 49) and Payne dates this pot type to IIIa. (1992, p. 188) There is nothing exactly like it in the Protodynastic Corpus.

Bibl:
Lowy catalog, p. 24, No. 29
Patch, 1991

STONE VASES

As the people of the Nile Valley moved out of the Paleolithic period into the Predynastic, their considerable skills in stone working developed ever further, leading to Egypt being called the "civilization of stone." (Shaw, p. 50) While their experience was primarily with flint formed into tools, they soon began to make stone vases. Stone vases required time and skill to craft and were considered luxury items. Their permanence made them especially valued for goods meant to accompany the deceased into the afterlife. Initially these vessels were small in size, often bulbous or cylindrical pots with rims and lug handles that appeared in burials, but only rarely. By mid-Nagada, c.3650 BCE, a wider range of stone was being worked (El-Kouli, 771, Holmes, 17) and the interiors were being drilled out more extensively. Eventually, in Nagada III, around 3000 BCE, a full range of material was being skillfully worked often in large size, and by the Early Dynastic period enormous, beautiful stone pots were made as temple offerings, replacing ceramics as the most luxurious grave goods. Like ceramic vases, the stone ones were intended to hold actual or symbolic contents (food, oils) necessary for the afterlife.

The vases started as a block of stone pounded with stone tools to form the rough shape. (El-Khouli, p. 791) Refined probably with metal saws and chisels, it would be smoothed with abrasive stones and sands. Once the exterior shape was finished, it would be hollowed out using a drill set with round or half-moon shaped bits made of flint, sandstone, limestone or diorite. (Holmes, 1989, pp. 308, 415,fig. 4) Finally the outside was polished using scraper stones and fine abrasives. There is an image in an Old Kingdom tomb relief showing a stone worker using a drill (probably with a flint bit) with stones arranged around the top as counterweights that could be swung around to give the drill the heft and momentum needed to carve out the stone, but it is unclear whether Old Kingdom technology was present in the Predynastic period. (El-Khouli, p. 789) The stone objects reveal the Egyptian artisan's ability to work extremely hard stone into delicately and perfectly formed shapes. The earlier pots are drilled straight down, so no matter what the outside shape, the inside one is cylindrical. Later they were able to drill out the inside of closed top vessels

Jeanne Ericson is responsible for much of this information. (Seminar Report, CSUSB, 2005)

45. *Stone Vase
Museum No. EI 01.001.2004

Height: 7 1/4" (18 cm .)
Rim exterior: 3 1/8" (7.8 cm.)
Rim width: 9/16" (1.3 cm.)
Greatest width: 4" (10 cm.)
Lug to lug: 4 3/16" (10.5 cm.)
Base: 1 15/16" (4.8 cm.)
Lug length: 2 7/8" (7.2 cm.), 2 3/4" ((6.8 cm.)
Lug thickness: 3/8" (.9 cm.)

Nagada IIc-IIIa1 c.3650-3200 BCE

Breccia (limestone)

While Egyptians used all sorts of stone, they always had a taste for veined or composite material which created a complex, variegated and visually interesting surface. Possibly the different kinds of stone had particular meanings.

Our pot is an excellent example of a soft, aggregate stone comprising a variety of materials, in this case with whitish beige occlusions in a reddish matrix. Aston, p. 54 gives a more detailed geological definition and identifies the sites where this stone was found. It seems that at first ceramics were the model for stone vases but later stone vases were copied in clay. A commonly held belief is that much of the Decorated ware with non-figurative images was imitating the pattern on stone vessels such as this one.

The overall shape is characteristic for stone vases: relatively tall, shouldered, closed [i.e. with the top opening smaller than the widest part of the vessel] (Aston, p. 179) with a round rim. It also has wide wavy lug handles that clearly copy those on Wavy-Handled ware, a type of ceramic vessel introduced in mid Nagada II (Kaiser, 1957, p. 72) although our pot seems to have flat handles with scalloped edges rather than a wavy shape. El-Khouli catalogs this type as a late Predynastic cylindrical jar with serpentine handles (1978, No. 1163, p. 771, pls. 47, 151), although his example is much smaller than ours. Our vessel is harmoniously proportioned with base to height of 1:4 and base to greatest width of 1:2 and it can stand on its base. The pot is heavy because not much material has been removed to form the interior, and two vertical holes were drilled at either end of each lug in order to attach a cord handle to facilitate its transport, or to hang it, just as they were on ceramic vessels. (Hope, 1982, p 30) Handles pierced this way appear on a stone vessel in the Brooklyn Museum. (Needler, 1984, p. 243). Such a device simplifies carrying a multitude of pots, and hanging a pot, even if stoppered, would add an additional element of safety from insects, vermin and children. It also gets the pot out of the way in what were probably cramped living conditions. However, a pot this heavy would present a danger should one accidentally bump against it, and its lug handles may also simply be a reference to a clay prototype.

The pot exemplifies the improving skills of the Egyptian stone workers, since its cavity is not just drilled straight down, creating a cylindrical inner shape, but has a curved interior shape like that of the exterior. On the interior, which is 6 1/8" deep, there are clear striations marks of the drilling tool used to create the interior space that tapers toward the bottom, where there is a slight conical indentation. The exterior is smooth.

Such skill is also witnessed by the size of this pot, which is large for its date. (Patch, personal communication) Nonetheless, it has an irregular, everted rim that dips to one side. It is not a perfectly symmetrical shape, being better balanced and finished at the bottom, but a bit off at the top where one side has a broader bulge. The result is that one ledge looks like it is higher than the other.

Both lugs are damaged, probably a sign of much usage.

Jeanne Ericson contributed substantially to this entry.

Date

El-Khouli (1978, p. 771) indicates that similar jars are found through the Predynastic with the serpentine handle indicating the late Predynastic and Dynasty I. Needler dates a similar breccia vase to Nagada II/III. (1984, p. 242, illustration on p. 243, pl. 29, No. 122). Ashton dates this type to Late Nagada II-Nagada III. (1994, p. 97, No. 19) Her example is shorter than ours, and the proportions are not exact, but the general shape is close. Patch dates this IId2-IIIa1, c.3300 BCE (personal communication).

Coll. Harer

Bibl:
El-Khouli, 1978
Needler, 1984
Ashton, 1994
Jeanne Ericson, Seminar Report, CSUSB, 2005

FLINT

Stone objects are the only material remains of humankind's earliest culture. They reveal human variety and development over hundreds of thousands of years. Even when new materials entered the tool repertory in the Neolithic, flint never died out, and in Predynastic times, along with clay, it was the most finely worked material for luxury goods, undoubtedly made by specialists. (Holmes, p. 337) The skill of the Predynastic flint nappers is extremely impressive, and while this skill declined during the Dynastic periods, flint never disappeared as a material for tools. It is a very common grave good, usually appearing at least once in almost every burial. (Patch, personal communication) The flint objects of the Eastern Sahara and the Nile Valley are key documents for historical investigations. Diane Holmes' study of stone materials from the early settlements of Upper Egypt (1989) revealed a complex picture of differing local communities, a major revision of previous evaluations of early Predynastic culture.

46. *Fish Tail Knife
Museum No. EI 01.015.1998

Nagada IIb-IId c.3650-3300 BCE

Length: 6 5/8" (16.5 cm.)
Width: 2" (5.1 cm.)
Depth of "V": 7/8" (2.2 cm.)
Thickness: 1/8" (.2 cm.)

Flint

Finely worked thin, delicate flint tools are hallmarks of the Predynastic period. One of the most characteristic examples is a beautifully made object called the "fishtail," a normally bifacial implement with a forked end, recalling the tail of a fish. (Holmes, 1989, p. 408) Our example was made of a beige flint with thin reddish veins running through it. Bahmer describes the "V" shape as the cutting end of this tool, with edges created by a second stage of flaking to produce the fine serrations with minuscule, exactingly regular teeth, which characterize these objects. (Holmes, 1989, 408) These serrations continue around almost the entire perimeter of the knife but vanish at the narrow point of the blade, which has been left rough and unfinished, also characteristic of the fishtail knives. (Holmes, ibid.)

The narrower end was meant for a handle. (Payne, 1993, p. 169) A fishtail from a Nagada grave was found with a cord wound around the haft end "with two alabaster knobs at the outer end, and the whole wrapped in hide." (Holmes, 1989, 408) This cord appears to have served as a haft. (Holmes, ibid.) A complete example was found at Naga ed Der with its blade sunk into a wooden handle, with a protective leather pouch. (Payne, 1993, p. 169) Examples of these objects have been found protectively bundled, with reed wrapping covering the cutting edge, wood hafts and leather binding – all indicating that they were ceremonial objects. (Patch, personal communication)

They were often found broken in graves, as if to "disarm" them in the afterlife. They are so finely made and have such a unique shape they must have had some special ceremonial significance. It resembles an instrument used in Dynastic times for the "opening of the mouth" ceremony involved with bringing life to the mummified remains of a deceased person and may have been a precursor to this instrument. (Payne, 1993, p. 169; Needler, p. 267, Roth, 1992) It is certainly an appropriate object to include in a grave. In the Old Kingdom the "Pss-Kf" instrument had a ritual function to insure that the newborn had the ability to take nourishment and by extension it helped the newly reborn deceased to eat the real and symbolic food provided in the funerary meal. (Roth, p. 147) Patch indicates that James Allen thinks it had medicinal uses, used to cut the umbilical cord after a birth. (Patch, personal communication)

There is a small break at the narrow end of this object.

Mieke Bahmer and Jeanne Ericson contributed substantially to this entry.

Date

Petrie illustrates a fishtail almost exactly the size of ours in Naqada and Ballas, 1896, pl.LXXIII, no.63. Kaiser, 1957, includes flint tools in his chronological scheme for the Predynastic and has a U-shaped knife in early Nagada (Ia, IIa and IIb). Holmes has refined the situation, indicating an earlier U-shaped fork from Nagada I and a V-shaped one from Nagada II. (Holmes 1989, pp. 16, 408) Kaiser illustrated the latter in Nagada IIb and mentioned finding one at Armant in level IIc. (Grave 1523) (1957, p. 72) Payne dates an example of almost the same size to IIb-IId. (1993, p. 169, fig. 66, cat. No. 1409) Needler (1984, p. 265) illustrates knives that she considers Badarian ancestors of the fishtail.

Coll. Harer

Bibl:
Kaiser, 1957
Needler, 1984
Holmes, 1989
Roth, 1992
Payne, 1993
Mieke Bahmer, Seminar Report, CSUSB, 2004
Jeanne Ericson, Seminar Report, CSUSB, 2005

BIBLIOGRAPHY

ADAMS, Barbara, Prehistoric Egypt, Aylesbury, 1988

ADAMS, Barbara, "Predynastic Pottery" in M.A. Hoffman, The First Egyptians, 1988, pp. 47-58

AKSAMIT, Joanna, "Petrie's Type D461 and Remarks on the Production and Decoration of Predynastic Pottery," Cahiers de la Céramique Égyptienne, 3, 1992, 17-21

ARKELL, A. J., "The Origin of Black-Topped Red Pottery," Journal of Egyptian Archaeology, 46, 1960, pp. 105-106

ARKELL, A.J. and Ucko, Peter J., "Review of Predynastic Development in the Nile Valley," Current Anthropology, Vol. 6, No. 2, 1965, pp. 145-166

ARKELL, A. J., The Prehistory of the Nile Valley, Leiden, 1975

ARNETT, W. S., The Predynastic Origins of Egyptian Hieroglyphics, Washington, D.C., 1982

ARNOLD, Dorothea and BOURRIAU, Janine, An Introduction to Ancient Egyptian Pottery, Mainz, 1993

ARNOLD, Dorothea, Studien zur Altägyptisches Keramik, Mainz, 1981

ASSELBERGHS, H., Chaos en Beheersing: Documenten uit Aeneolithisch Egypte, Leiden, 1961

ASTON, Barbara, Ancient Egyptian Stone Vessels – Materials and Forms, Heidelberg, 1994

AYRTON, E. R. and W. L. S. LOAT, The Pre-dynastic Cemetery at El-Mahasna, London, 1911

BABA, Masahiro and SAITO, Mansanori, "Experimental Studies on the Firing Methods of the Black-Topped Pottery in Predynastic Egypt, " in Ciałowicz, 2002, pp. 10-11

BARD, Kathryn A., From Farmers to Pharaohs Mortuary Evidence for the Rise of Complex Society in Egypt, Sheffield, 1994

BAUMGARTEL, Elise, The Cultures of Predynastic Egypt I, 2nd rev.ed., London, 1955

BAUMGARTEL, Elise, The Cultures of Predynastic Egypt II, London, 1960

BEHRMANN, A., "Zur Bedeutung der Nilpferd-Fayencen," Göttinger Miszellen, 96, 1987, pp. 11-22

BEHRMANN, A., Das Nilpferd in der Vorstellungswelt der Alten Ägypter, Teil I, Katalog, Frankfurt am Main, 1989

BOURRIAU, Janine, Umm El-Ga'ab Pottery from the Nile Valley before the Arab Conquest, Cambridge, 1981

BRACK, A. and H. ZOLLER, "Die Pflanze auf der dekorierten Naqada-II Keramik: Aloe oder Wildbanane (Ensete?)" Mitteilungen des Deutschen Archäologischen Instituts, Abteilung Kairo, 45, 1989 ,33-53 cited in El Hadidi.

BREWER, D. J. and Renée FRIEDMAN, Fish and Fishing in Ancient Egypt, Warminster, 1989

BRUNTON, Guy and Gertrude CATON-THOMPSON, The Badarian Civilisation, London, 1928

CALINESCU, Irena, Object Examination Reports, March 7 – April 25, 2005 (on file in Robert V. Fullerton Art Museum, California State University, San Bernardino)

CIAŁOWICZ, Krzysztof M., CHŁODNICKI, Marek and HENDRICKX, Stan (eds.), Origin of the State. Predynastic and Early Dynastic Egypt, Cracow, 2002 (Abstracts)

DE MORGAN, Jacques, Recherches sur les Origines de l'Égypte, I L'age de la Pierre et des métaux, Paris, 1896

DE MORGAN, Jacques, Recherches sur les Origines de l'Égypte, II Ethnographie préhistorique et tombeau royal de Négadah, Paris, 1897

EL HADIDI, Nabil "Notes on Egyptian Weeds of Antiquity: I. Min's Lettuce and the Naqada Plant," in Friedman and Adams, 1992, 323-326

EL KHOULI, Ali, Egyptian Stone Vessels Predynastic Period to Dynasty III, Vols. I-III, Mainz, 1978

EL-YAHKY, Farid, "Remarks on the Armless Human Figures Represented on Gerzean Boats," Journal of the Society for the Study of Egyptian Antiquities, Vol. 11, No. 2, 1981, pp. 77-84

EL-YAHKY, Farid, "The Origin and Development of Sanctuaries in Predynastic Egypt,"Journal of the Society for the Study of Egyptian Antiquities, Vol. 14, No. 3, 1984, pp. 70-73

EL-YAHKY, Farid, "Clarifications on the Gerzean Boat Scenes," Bulletin de l'Institut français d'archéologie orientale, Vol. 85, 1985, pp. 187-195

ENDESFELDER, Erika, "Zur Keramikausstattung Prädynastischer Gräber", Meroitica, Vol. 12, 1990, pp. 97-118

ENGELBACH, R., Harageh, 1923

FAIRSERVIS, W. A., Hierakonpolis – The Graffiti and the Origins of Egyptian Hieroglyphic Writing. The Hierakonpolis Project. Occasional Papers in Anthropology 2. Poughkkeepsie, N.Y., 1983, cited in Finkenstaedt, 1985, p. 85.

FINKENSTAEDT, Elizabeth, "The Internal Chronology of Egyptian Predynastic Black-Topped Ware," American Journal of Archaeology, 1974, p. 165

FINKENSTAEDT, Elizabeth, "The Chronology of Egyptian Black-Topped Ware," Zeitschrift für Ägyptische Sprache und Altertumskunde, 103, 1976, pp. 5-8

FINKENSTAEDT, Elizabeth, "Regional Painting Style in Prehistoric Egypt, " Zeitschrift für Ägyptische Sprache und Altertumskunde, 107, 1980, pp. 116-120

FINKENSTAEDT, Elizabeth, "The Location of Styles in Painting: White Cross-Lined Ware at Naqada," Journal of the American Research Center in Egypt, 18, 1981, pp. 7-10

FINKENSTAEDT, Elizabeth, "Cognitive vs. Ecological Niches in Prehistoric Egypt, " Journal of the American Research Center in Egypt, XXII, 1985, pp. 143-147

FINKENSTAEDT, Elizabeth, "Prehistoric Egyptian Pottery," The Bulletin of the Cleveland Museum of Art, Vol. 75, No. 3, 1985, pp. 75-94

FINKENSTAEDT, Elizabeth, "On the Life-Span of Decorated Ware in the Gerzean Period, Zeitschrift für Ägyptische Sprache und Altertumskunde, 112, 1985, pp. 17-19

FRIEDMAN, Renée, Spatial Distribution in a Predynastic Cemetery: Naga ed Der 7000, M.A. Thesis, Berkeley, University of California, 1981 (not seen)

FRIEDMAN, Renée and ADAMS, Barbara, Followers of Horus, Exeter, 1992

FRIEDMAN, Renée, Predynastic Settlement Ceramics of Upper Egypt: A Comparative Study of the Ceramics of Hememieh, Nagada, and Hierakonpolis, Ph.D. Thesis, Berkeley, University of California, 1994

GAMER-WALLERT, Ingrid, Fische und Fischkulte im Alten Ägypten, Wiesbaden, 1970

GELLER, J.R., The Predynastic Ceramic Industry at Hierakonpolis Egypt, M.A. Thesis, St. Louis, Washington University, 1984

GELLER, J.R., "Recent Excavations at Hierakonpolis and their Relevance to Predynastic Production and Settlement," Cahier de recherches de l'Institut de papyrologie et d'égyptologie de Lille, Vol. 11, 1989, pp. 41-52

GEORGE, Beate, Frühe Keramik aus Agyptien Die Dekorierte Negade II-Keramik im Medelhavmuseet, Stockholm, 1975

GRAFF, Gwenola, "Les peintures sur vases Nagada I-II. Nouvelle approche sémiologique," in Ciałowicz, 2002, pp. 37-38

GRAFF, Gwenola, "Les vases nagadiens comportant des représentations d'addax," Cahiers Caribéens d'Egyptologie, no. 5, fev-mars, 2003, pp. 35-57

HASSAN, F. A., "Radiocarbon Chronology of Predynastic Naqada Settlements, Egypt", Current Anthropology, 25, 1984, pp. 681-683

HENDRICKX, Stan, De grafvelden der Naqada-cultuur in Zuid-Egypte, met bijzondere aandache voor het Naqada III grafveld te Elkab. Interne chronologie en sociale differentiatie, Ph.D. Thesis, Leuven, 1989 (not seen)

HENDRICKX, Stan, Analytical Bibliography of the Prehistory and the Early Dynastic Period of Egypt and Northern Sudan, Leuven, 1995

HENDRICKX, Stan, "The Relative Chronology of the Naqada Culture: Problems and Possibilities," in Spencer, 1996, pp. 36-69

HENDRICKX, Stan, "Peaux d'animaux comme symbols prédynastiques," Chronique d'Égypte, v. 73, 1998, pp. 203-230

HENDRICKX, Stan, "La chronologie de la préhistoire tardive et des débuts de l'histoire de l'Egypte," Archéo-Nil, 9, 1999, pp. 13-81

HENDRICKX, Stan, "Review of Wilkinson's 'State Formation in Egypt, Chronology and Society'," The Journal of Egyptian Archaeology, 86, 1999, pp.241-245

HENDRICKX, Stan, "Autruches et flamants – les oiseaux représentés sur la céramique prédynastique de la catégorie Decorated," Cahiers Caribéens d'Egyptologie, no. 1, 2000, pp. 21-52

HENDRICKX, Stan and DEPRAETERE, David, "A Theriomorphic Predynastic Stone Jar and Hippopotamus Symbolism," in S. Hendrickx, Freidman, R. F., Ciałowicz, K.M. and Chłodnicki, M. (eds.), Egypt at its Origins. Studies in Memory of Barbara Adams, Proceedings of the International Conference "Origins of the State; Predynastic and Early Dynastic Egypt," (Krakow 2002), Leuven, 2004 (12 page email version)

HENDRICKX, Stan, Predynastic – Early Dynastic Chronology, 2005 (e-mail version sent to author, 26pp.)

HODGES, Henry, "Black-Topped Pottery, an Empirical Study", Bulletin de liaison du Groupe international pour l'étude de la céramique égyptienne, v. 7, 1982, pp. 45-51

HOFFMAN, Michael Allen, The Predynastic of Hierakonpolis – An Interim Report, Egyptian Studies Association Publication, No. 1, Giza and McComb, 1982

HOFFMAN, Michael Allen, The First Egyptians, 1988

HOFFMAN, Michael Allen, Egypt Before the Pharoahs, New York, 1993 (orig. 1979)

HOLMES, Diane L., The Predynastic Lithic Industries of Upper Egypt, Cambridge, 1989

HOPE, Colin A., Ancient Egyptian Pottery, Melbourne, 1982

KAISER, Werner, "Zur inneren Chronologie der Naqada Kultur," Archaeologia Geographica, 6, 1957, pp. 69-77

KELLEY, A. L., The Pottery of Ancient Egypt, Dynasty I to Roman Times, Toronto, 1976

KEMP, Barry , Ancient Egypt. Anatomy of a Civilization, London, 1974

KEMP, Barry, "Automatic Analysis of Predynastic Cemeteries: A New Method for an Old Problem," Journal of Egyptian Archaeology, 68, 1982, pp. 5-15

KROEPER, Karla, "Minshat Abu Omar – Burials with Palettes" in Spencer, 1996, pp. 70-92

KRYZANIAK, L. and KOBUSIEWICZ, M., Late Prehistory of the Nile Basin and the Sahara, Poznan, 1989

LACOVARA, Peter, "A New Date for an Old Hippopotamus," Journal of the Museum of Fine Arts, Boston, Vol. 4, 1992, pp. 17-26

LOWY CATALOG (Anonymous manuscript in the files of the Robert V. Fullerton Art Museum, California State University, San Bernardino)

MIDANT-REYNES, et. al, "The Predynastic Site of Adaima: Settlement and Cemetery," in Spencer, 1996, pp. 93-97

MIDANT-REYNES, Beatrix, The Prehistory of Egypt, London, 2000

MILLETT, Martin, "An Approach to the Functional Interpretation of Pottery" in M. Millett, ed., Pottery and the Archaeologist, Occasional Publication No. 4, Institute of Archaeology, London, 1979

MOND, Sir Robert and Oliver H. MYERS, Cemeteries of Armant I and II, London, 1937

MONET-SALEH, Janine, "Forteresses, ou Villes-Protégées thinites?," Bulletin de l'Institut francais d'archéologie orientale, Vol. 67, 1969, 173-187

MONET-SALEH, Janine, "Les Représentations de Temples sur Plates-Formes à Pieux de la Poterie Gerzéenne d'Egypte," Bulletin de l'Institut francais d'archéologie orientale, Vol. 83, 1983, pp. 263-296

NAVILLE, Edouard, "La Poterie Primitive en Egypt," L'Anthropologie, Vol. 23, 1912, pp. 313-320

NAVILLE, Edouard, "Les dessins des vases préhistoriques égyptiens," Archives suisses d'anthropologie, Vol. 2, Issue 1-2, 1916/17, pp. 77-82

NAVILLE, Edouard, "Les dessins des vases préhistoriques égyptiens II", Archives suisses d'anthropologie, Vol. 4, Issue 3, 1921, pp. 197-206

NEEDLER, Winifred, "Federn's Revision of Petrie's Predynastic Classification," Journal of the Society for the Study of Egyptian Antiquities, VII, 1981, pp. 69-74

NEEDLER, Winifred, Predynastic and Archaic Egypt in the Brooklyn Museum, Brooklyn, 1984

NORDSTROM, Hans-Ake, Neolithic and A Group Sites, Stockholm, 1972

PATCH, Diana, The Origin and Early Development of Urbanism in Ancient Egypt: A Regional Study, Ph.D. Thesis, Philadelphia, University of Pennsylvania, 1991

PAYNE, J. Crowfoot, "Forged Decoration on Predynastic Pots," Journal of Egyptian Archaeology, 63, 1977, pp. 5-12

PAYNE, J. Crowfoot,, "The Chronology of Predynastic Egyptian Decorated Ware," Eretz Yisrael, 21, 1990, pp. 77-82

PAYNE, J. Crowfoot, "Predynastic Chronology at Naqada" in Friedman, R. and B. Adams, 1992, pp. 185-192

PAYNE, J. Crowfoot, Catalogue of the Predynastic Egyptian Collection in the Ashmolean Museum, Oxford, 1993

PETRIE, W. M. Flinders, Naqada and Ballas, London, 1896 (reprint Warminster, 1974)

PETRIE, W. M. Flinders, Diospolis Parva, London, 1901, frontispiece

PETRIE, W. M. Flinders, Prehistoric Egypt - Corpus of Prehistoric Pottery and Palettes, London, 1921

PETRIE, W. M. Flinders, The Making of Egypt, London, 1939

PETRIE, W. M. Flinders, Corpus of Proto Dynastic Pottery, 1953

RIZKANA, Ibrahim and Jurgen SEEHER, Maadi I. The Pottery of the Predynastic Settlement, Mainz am Rhein, 1987

ROTH, Anne Macy, "The PSS-KF and the 'Opening of the Mouth' Ceremony: A Ritual of Birth and Rebirth," Journal of Egyptian Archaeology, 78, 1992, pp. 133-147

SCHARFF, Alexander, Die Altertümer der Vor- und Frühzeit Ägyptens, Berlin, 1931

SCOTT, Gerry D., III, Ancient Egyptian Art at Yale, New Haven, Yale University Art Gallery, 1986

SCOTT, Gerry D., III, Temple, Tomb and Dwelling: Egyptian Antiquities from the Harer Family Trust Collection, San Bernardino, 1992

SHAW, Ian, The Oxford History of Ancient Egypt, Oxford, 2000

SMITH, A. L., "Identification d'un Potier Prédynastique," Archéo-Nil, 3, 1993, pp. 23-33

SPENCER, A. J., Early Egypt, Norman, 1993

SPENCER, Jeffrey, Aspects of Early Egypt, London, 1996

TRIGGER, B.G. et. al, Ancient Egypt A Social History, Cambridge, 1983

VAN DEN BRINK, E. C. M., "Corpus and Numerical Evaluation of the 'Thinite' Potmarks," in Friedman and Adams, 1992, pp. 265 - 296

VANDIER, Jacques, L'Egypte avant les pyramides, Paris, 1973

WENKE, Robert J., "The Evolution of Early Egyptian Civilization: Issues and Evidence," Journal of World Prehistory, Vol. 5, no. 3, 1991, pp. 179-219

WILDUNG, Dietrich, Ägypten Vor den Pyramiden, Mainz, 1981

WILKINSON, Toby A.H., A New Comparative Chronology for the Predynastic-Early Dynastic Transition, Journal of the Ancient Chronology Forum, vol. 7, 1994/1995, pp. 5-26

WILKINSON, Toby A.H., State Formation in Egypt, Chronology and Society, Oxford, 1996

WILKINSON, Toby A.H., Early Dynastic Egypt, London and New York, 1999

WILKINSON, Toby A.H., "Political Unification: towards a reconstruction," Mitteilungen des Deutschen Archäologischen Instituts, Abteilung Kairo, 56, 2000, pp. 377-395

WILKINSON, Toby, Genesis of the Pharaohs, London, 2003

WILLIAMS, Bruce and LOGAN, Thomas J. "The Metropolitan Knife Handle and Aspects of Pharaonic Imagery Before Narmer," Journal of Near Eastern Studies, v. 46, n. 4, 1987, pp. 245-285

WILLIAMS, Bruce, Decorated Pottery and the Art of Nagada III, Munich, 1988